Patrons and Painters:
Art in Scotland 1650–1760

Sponsored by ✸ **The Royal Bank of Scotland**

in association with

D1439549

Patrons and Painters
Art in Scotland 1650–1760

James Holloway

Scottish National Portrait Gallery

Published by the Trustees of the National Galleries of Scotland to accompany the exhibition *Patrons and Painters: Art in Scotland 1650–1760*, held at the Scottish National Portrait Gallery, 17 July to 8 October 1989.

The front cover reproduces Apelles and Campaspe [25] *by Sir John de Medina, the back cover Richard Waitt's* Self-portrait [62]

ISBN 0 903148 89 7

Designed by Cinamon and Kitzinger
Typeset by Wyvern Typesetting Ltd
Printed by Alna Press Ltd

Contents

Foreword   page 7
Introduction   page 9

David Scougal, Jacob de Wet,
John Michael Wright
and the patronage of the
Royal House of Stewart   *page 13*

Sir John de Medina,
William Gouw Ferguson,
John Scougal
and the patronage of the
Earls of Leven and Melville   *page 33*

William Aikman, James Norie
and the patronage of
John, 2nd Duke of Argyll   *page 51*

Richard Waitt, John Smibert
and the patronage of
Clan Grant   *page 69*

John Alexander, William Mosman
and the patronage of the
Duffs and Gordons   *page 85*

Academies, societies
and the patronage of the
City of Edinburgh   *page 105*

Allan Ramsay
and the patronage of
John, 3rd Earl of Bute   *page 123*

Notes   *page 139*
Artists' biographies   *page 140*
Select bibliography   *page 150*
Index of Artists and Architects   *page 151*
Lenders   *page 152*

Foreword

Unlike most public art collections, assembled to display the talents of painters, the chief purpose of the Scottish National Portrait Gallery is to present the features of men and women of reputation. Entry is by virtue of historical importance rather than artistic excellence, though the collection's greatest portraits combine both qualities.

Because portraiture dominated British art until the mid-nineteenth century, the Portrait Gallery contains the first of the three volumes of the history of Scottish art, of which the second and third are displayed at the National Gallery and at the Gallery of Modern Art. *Patrons and Painters: Art in Scotland 1650–1760* examines several chapters of this first volume, a neglected period in Scottish art. Patronage as much as painting is its subject, a wholly novel approach, but a particularly appropriate one, considering the dual nature of the Portrait Gallery itself.

1989 is the centenary of the Scottish National Portrait Gallery. It was John Ritchie Findlay, senior proprietor of *The Scotsman* newspaper, who gave the money to build and endow the Gallery. It is consequently a great source of pleasure that our links with *The Scotsman* have continued and that it is supporting our centenary celebrations.

The exhibition has been generously sponsored by another old friend of the National Galleries, the Royal Bank of Scotland. It is rather older than we are, having been founded in 1727. One of its first employees, later the Chief Cashier, was John Campbell of the Bank, whose elegant portrait by William Mosman has been lent by the bank.

The Royal Bank of Scotland is one of a large number of generous lenders, public and private, who have stripped their walls to enhance ours. In every instance our requests have been met with generosity. Scotland is fortunate and unusual in that so many family portraits still hang in the houses for which they were painted. The Scottish National Portrait Gallery is grateful for the readiness of their owners to share them with us.

TIMOTHY CLIFFORD
Director of the National
Galleries of Scotland

DUNCAN THOMSON
Keeper of the Scottish
National Portrait Gallery

Introduction

Most exhibitions which set out to survey the art of a country or region tend to follow a familiar and well-established pattern. The artists are considered chronologically, in isolation from the events of their time and with little reference to the aspirations of the men and women who commissioned their work. There are advantages in this method, particularly when the artists themselves are well-known and when their work, looked at together, can be seen to share certain characteristics and form a distinctive school of art.

This exhibition takes a somewhat different approach. The articulation is provided by a number of families (and one city) and the artists are discussed in the context of the patronage of these families. One of the main reasons for departing from the usual practice is that the families I have selected are still, by and large, well-known in Scotland, whereas for all but one or two major figures, the artists have been forgotten.

The activities of the different families provide, I hope, the historical and cultural background against which the art of the period can be seen more fully. They have been selected to provide a contrast of religious and political opinion, financial and social standing, and geographical location. The exhibition opens with the royal court at Holyroodhouse in the first chapter, moves round the country to the West, to the Highlands, and to the North-East, before returning to Edinburgh in the penultimate chapter. The exhibition ends once more at court, but with Scottish artists based in London.

The concentration on just a few families has meant the exclusion of others. That the Dukes of Atholl or Queensberry are hardly mentioned is not meant to imply that they were inactive, merely that it suited my purpose in unravelling the art of the period to spotlight others.

I have received much help and kindness during the preparation of this exhibition which I should like to acknowledge. It was Dr Duncan Thomson who, fourteen years ago, as Assistant Keeper of the Scottish National Portrait Gallery, arranged the exhibition *Painting in Scotland 1570–1650*. Now, Keeper of the Gallery, he encouraged me to organise the successor to his exhibition, and he has been generous in allowing me time for research and writing.

Patrons and Painters: Art in Scotland 1650–1760 explores a neglected area of British art, and my task would have been almost impossible, certainly impracticably lengthy, had it not been for the work of my colleagues, past and present. They have built up the archive of the Scottish National Portrait Gallery into an indispensable research facility, and I should like to thank Dr Rosalind Marshall, who runs it, and my other colleagues, Helen Smailes and Sara Stevenson, for their continuous helpfulness and advice.

No one working on eighteenth-century Scottish art underestimates the contribution made by Basil Skinner, my predecessor as Assistant Keeper. His many discoveries, modestly filed away into the anonymity of the archive or accession envelope, I have eagerly seized and published. Tristram Clarke and Peter Vasey at the Scottish Record Office, Iain Brown and Alastair Cherry at the National Library, Kitty Cruft and Neil Cameron at the Royal Commission on the Ancient and Historical Monuments of Scotland, Rab Snowden at Stenhouse Conservation, David Walker and Aonghus MacKechnie at Historic Buildings and Monuments, and Elizabeth Roads at the Court of the Lord Lyon have all been ready to answer questions. Ian Gow and Richard Emerson have been particular allies, answering my many importunate enquiries with unfailing tolerance and speed. I should like to thank too Janis Adams of our publications department, Lindsay Errington at the National Gallery, John Dick at Belford Road, and Charles Burnett at the Castle. Hugh Cheape, of the National Museums of Scotland, has readily shared his extensive knowledge of Highland life.

In London Elizabeth Einberg at the Tate Gallery, Antony Griffiths at the British Museum, and Mary Cosh have each been generous with their time. With the assistance of Kim Sloan I was fortunate enough to be able to consult the invaluable papers of Sir Brinsley Ford, which are now deposited at the Paul Mellon Centre in London. In Washington, Cecilia Chin gave me access to the archives and libraries of the National Portrait Gallery and Smithsonian Institution, and with her help, and that of Ellen Miles and Richard Saunders, I was able to gather much information on Scottish artists in America. I met with similar kindness at the Rijksbureau voor Kunsthistorische Documentatie at The Hague and from Anne Crookshank in Dublin.

Certain people were particularly helpful on individual artists: P. A. Hopkins on the iconography of the Warrender still-life, for instance. With Alastair Smart I was able to discuss Allan Ramsay, an artist he has made his own. We looked at portraits together and I learnt much from his observations and discussions.

Finally I should like to thank the photographers and typists who have worked alongside me: of the former, Jack Mackenzie, Antonia Reeve and Ian Larner, also Susanna Kerr, who has co-ordinated their work. Sheila Smith and Alison Boocock have had the unenviable job of reading my handwriting and typing my manuscript.

JAMES HOLLOWAY

David Scougal, Jacob de Wet, John Michael Wright and the patronage of the Royal House of Stewart

On 1 January 1651 Charles II was crowned King of Scots at Scone. He had arrived in the country the previous summer in an attempt to win back the thrones of Scotland and England, lost when his father was executed at White-hall. Charles's time in Scotland was short. In August he and his army crossed the border into England. He was defeated at the battle of Worcester and fortunate in managing to escape once more to the Continent. The thirteen months he spent in Scotland cannot have been particularly pleasant ones. On the run from Cromwell, lectured at by the Presbyterians, who had made acceptance of the National Covenant and parliamentary government a condition of their support, it is all the more surprising that he had time to patronise the arts and to appoint a King's Limner in Scotland, the painter David Des Granges.

Des Granges is best-known as a miniaturist. He painted oil portraits as well, though none of these is known to date from his short stay in Scotland. The miniature of Charles II [1], signed and dated 1651, was one of the works Des Granges painted in Scotland but for which he had still not received payment twenty years later. In November 1671 he petitioned the King, stating that he was 'old & infirm, & his sight & labour failing him'. He had 'served your Majesty faithfully & diligently before your restauration as your limner in Scotland, on accompt of which service there became due to your petitioner the summ of threescore & sixteen pounds for several pieces of work by him done & delivered to sundry persons of quality by Your Majesties own hands or your express order.'[1]

Des Granges's miniature, adapted from Adriaen Hanne-man's oil portrait, became Charles's official image,

13

I

DAVID DES GRANGES

Charles II (1630–85)

Signed and dated: DDG 1651
Watercolour on vellum
1⅞ x 1½ (4.8 x 3.8)*
C. Cottrell-Dormer Esq.

This miniature, based on Hanneman's portrait of the King, which was painted in The Hague about two years earlier, could be the work described in Des Granges's petition of 1671: 'One picture of yoʳ Majᵗʸ in small, delivered to the French Marquess who came to yoʳ Majᵗʸ at St Johnston's [Perth] in 1651'.

*Dimensions are given in inches followed by centimetres in parentheses.

14

presented by him to ambassadors, courtiers and supporters. What happened to Des Granges immediately after 1651 is not known. It is likely that he followed the King.

It is not perhaps surprising, given the unsettled state of the country in the aftermath of civil war, that little is known about the artists of the mid-century. It is recorded that Isaac Visitella lived in the Canongate, where he died in 1657. His will lists portraits of the Earls of Caithness and Winton amongst others, but no work by him can be identified today.

One painter of quality who did emerge during the 1650s was David Scougal. Among the first portraits he painted was one of Archibald Campbell, Marquis of Argyll, the man who had crowned Charles king at Scone [2]. Known familiarly in the Gaelic-speaking world as Gilleasbeg Gruamach for his squint, Argyll long held a dominant role in Scottish politics until, in May 1661, he died on the scaffold on the orders of King Charles II. Scougal's portrait, which neither flatters his appearance nor underestimates his intelligence, is unlikely to be posthumous.

The portrait of the Marquis is not signed or dated, but it is first recorded in an inventory of c. 1720 with an attribution to David Scougal, which is likely to be correct. Argyll's daughter Jean was also painted by Scougal, the only portrait to survive which is signed. It is also dated 1654, earlier than any other portrait attributed to him [3].

With these two as yardsticks, and with others attributable to David Scougal on documentary evidence, a group of portraits can be attributed to him which date from the mid-1650s to the late 1670s. Early in his career, dating from 1656, is the portrait of David, 2nd Earl of Wemyss. His countess and third wife, Margaret Leslie, was painted in the following year. To 1658 belongs the pair of portraits of James Grant of Freuchie and his wife. A characteristic of the male portraits of the 1650s is the way the artist modelled his heads out of angled planes, accentuating the cheek-bone. His women have softer features. Often very similar jewelry appears on different sitters, for instance the necklace and eardrops that are worn by the Duchess of Rothes [6] and Lady Clerk of Penicuik [7]. David Scougal's later portraits of men, for instance the young Lord Oxfuird, of 1666 [4], or Sir John Clerk of Penicuik, of 1674 [5], are more refined than his earlier male portraits, the artist having learnt to soften his modelling without losing his ability to portray intelligence and character. It has been suggested that David Scougal studied under John Michael Wright. He certainly copied his work, as he did Van Dyck's; but perhaps it was just that familiarity with more sophisticated portraiture improved the quality of his own painting.

2

DAVID SCOUGAL

Archibald Campbell, Marquis of
Argyll (1598–1661)

Oil on canvas
29 x 26½ (73.7 x 67.3)
Scottish National Portrait Gallery

*This portrait is first recorded in an
inventory of Newbattle Abbey of about
1720. It was listed as by David Scougal.
The portrait probably dates from the last
decade of the sitter's life.*

3

DAVID SCOUGAL

Lady Jean Campbell
(c. 1644–1700)

Signed and dated: Dᵈ Soŭgall
Anno 1654
Oil on panel
8½ x 6⅞ (21.6 x 17.4)
Scottish National Portrait Gallery

*The daughter of the Marquis of Argyll
[2], Lady Jean married the Earl of
Lothian in 1661 but died the year before
the Lothian earldom was raised to a
marquisate. The signature on this
portrait is like David Scougal's known
signature and, although previously doub-
ted, is likely to be authentic. There is no
reason either to dispute the date of 1654.
It follows that this portrait is the earliest
surviving work of David Scougal, the
only work by him to be signed and a rare
survival of what may not have been
unusual in his oeuvre, small cabinet-
sized portraits.*

15

4

DAVID SCOUGAL

Robert Macgill, 2nd Viscount
Oxfuird (1651–1705)

Oil on canvas
30 x 25 (76.2 x 63.5)
Private collection

The portrait is incorrectly inscribed 'Sir
Peter Lely pinxᵗ'. A document dated
Edinburgh, 8 September 1666, refers to
a payment of '8 rex dollars by the
Viscount of Oxford's order to be given to
David Scougal painter, for drawing the
said noble Viscount's portrait of him.'
This is likely to be the portrait. The sitter
was also a patron of Jacob de Wet.

5

DAVID SCOUGAL

Sir John Clerk of Penicuik, Bt
(1649–1722)

Oil on canvas
30 x 25 (76.2 x 63.5)
Sir John Clerk of Penicuik, Bt

The Clerk of Penicuik account book
records a payment to Mr Scougal of £58
in May 1674 'for my wyfes pictures and
mine.' If, as seems likely, that refers to the
payment for [5] and [7], they may be
among David Scougal's last works. Con-
fusion has been caused by a later payment
of £36 (November 1675) 'to John Scou-
gall for 2 pictures'; hitherto an attribu-
tion to John Scougal of these portraits has
been traditional. Yet there is no reason
why the Scougals should have been paid
twice for the same pair of portraits, which
in any case look quite unlike the
documented work of John Scougal.

6

DAVID SCOUGAL

Anne, Duchess of Rothes
(dates not known)

Oil on canvas
28¾ x 23½ (73.0 x 59.7)
The Rt Honble the Earl of Rothes

*The portrait is neither signed nor dated
but is entirely characteristic of the work of
David Scougal. The brooch, pearl necklace and eardrops appear in several of his
other portraits (e.g. Lady Nairne and
Agnes Wilkie). The sitter, a daughter of
John, 17th Earl of Crawford, married
the Earl, later Duke, of Rothes in 1648.*

7

DAVID SCOUGAL

Elizabeth Henderson, Lady Clerk
(died 1683)

Oil on canvas
30 x 25 (76.2 x 63.5)
Sir John Clerk of Penicuik, Bt

*[5] and [7] are a pair and were probably
marriage portraits. Elizabeth Henderson was also painted by Jacob de Wet.*

8

JOHN MICHAEL WRIGHT

Astraea Returns to Earth

Oil on canvas
90 x 56 (228.6 x 142.2) oval
Nottingham Castle Museum and
Art Gallery

*Painted for the ceiling of King Charles's
bedchamber in Whitehall. The subject,
from Ovid's* Metamorphoses, *alludes to
the Restoration of the King. Astraea, the
personification of Justice, fled the earth
with the onset of the Age of Iron; her
return, announced on the banner 'Terras
Astraea Revisit', heralded a new Golden
Age.*

John Michael Wright was born in London in 1617, very
likely to Scottish parents. He moved to Edinburgh in 1636
to begin an apprenticeship with George Jamesone, and he
probably remained in the city until at least 1641. Wright
subsequently travelled to Rome and later worked in the
Low Countries, London and Dublin. It is not known
whether the many Scottish sitters whom he painted sat in
London or whether the artist ever visited Scotland again.
  Soon after the Restoration of Charles II in 1660 Wright
gained royal attention and patronage, which he retained
intermittently until Charles's brother James VII fled
Britain in 1688. One of his earliest royal commissions was
for the ceiling in the King's bedchamber at Whitehall
Palace [8]. Wright was given as his subject the story from
Ovid of Astraea's return to earth after the horrors of the

9
JOHN MICHAEL WRIGHT
King Charles II (1630–85)
Oil on canvas
25⅛ x 31⅛ (63.8 x 79.0)
The Rt Honble the Earl of
Wemyss and March, K.T.

Age of Iron, drawing the parallel with Charles's own return to Britain after the Commonwealth and Protectorate. The ceiling reveals how much Wright learnt from his eight years in Italy, where he had been a member of the prestigious Roman Academy of St Luke. It is the most accomplished and thoroughgoing baroque decoration painted by a British artist, though Wright's Astraea has more in common with the ceilings of Andrea Sacchi and Pietro da Cortona, a generation older, than with the ceilings of his Roman contemporaries.

For Queen Catherine of Braganza's privy chamber Wright painted, appropriately, a chimneypiece depicting St Catherine. It may have been commissioned in 1662, the year the Queen arrived in London. His impressive portrait of the King shows Charles II enthroned wearing the St Edward's crown and holding the orb and sceptre made for the coronation of 1661 [*10*]. It is an unusually hierarchic image for a mid-seventeenth-century royal portrait, recalling Tudor, or even medieval, images of royalty, perhaps deliberately to stress the antiquity of the monarchy. It might be expected that the painting was made at the time of the English coronation in April 1661, but in a letter

Unrecorded in the literature, this portrait of the King appears to be the sketch for [10]. It is possible that it might originally have been painted with a Scottish destination in mind.

10

JOHN MICHAEL WRIGHT

King Charles II (1630–85)

Oil on canvas

111½ x 94¾ (283.2 x 240.7)

By Gracious Permission of Her
Majesty The Queen

*This very large and impressive portrait
shows the King enthroned as head of
state. It may have been sent to Rome in
1686 with the embassy that Wright
stage-managed for the Earl of Castlemaine. The portrait, or a version of it,
appears in van Westerhout's engraving
of Lord Castlemaine's great banquet in
the Palazzo Doria-Pamphilii.*

written in July 1676 Wright states that 'The King will sitt
to my great picture for the citty this next mon(e)th'. If
Wright's comment refers to this portrait, then the commission may have come from Sir Robert Vyner, the
prominent London goldsmith, who had made the regalia
for the coronation, had commissioned an equestrian
statue of Charles II, and had, already in the 1670s, sat to
Wright with his family and ordered from him a portrait of
Prince Rupert.

The recently discovered oil sketch [9] does not help to
answer the problem of date or patron. If anything it adds
an element of confusion. Charles seems slightly younger
in the sketch and the coat of arms behind him, a prominent
and important part of the image, is quartered differently,
with the arms of Scotland, not France and England, as in
the large painting, in the first (most important) quarter. It
would be interesting to know whether the King intended
Wright to paint his portrait for Holyroodhouse, the
palace of his Stewart ancestors.

Throughout the 1670s Wright styled himself 'Pictor
Regius', the King's painter, but unlike his great contemporary Sir Peter Lely, he received neither a knight-
hood nor the position and salary of Principal Painter. At

II

JOHN MICHAEL WRIGHT

John Leslie, Duke of Rothes
(1630–81)

Oil on canvas
49¾ x 40¾ (126.4 x 103.5)
The Rt Honble the Earl of Rothes

Probably painted in the mid-1660s, when Rothes's political influence was at its height. This portrait, with its well-observed and individual head and colour scheme of silver, black and pink, is one of Wright's finest works.

Fig. 1
John Maitland, Duke of Lauderdale, by Sir Peter Lely. Scottish National Portrait Gallery

12
DAVID PATON
The Yester Lords
Plumbago on vellum
5½ x 6⅜ (14.0 x 16.2)
National Gallery of Scotland

Neither the attribution to Paton nor the identity of the two men is certain. The latter have traditionally been called the Yester Lords, and it has been suggested that the drawing portrays the 1st Marquis of Tweeddale and his brother William Hay of Drummelzier.

his finest, Wright was a worthy rival of Lely, yet they were very different artists, Wright reticent and detached, Lely confident and assured, the heir of Van Dyck. Their respective strengths and differences can be seen clearly in their portraits of the two leading Scottish politicians of the early Restoration. As a man of twenty the Earl of Rothes had carried the Sword of State at Charles's Scottish coronation [*11*]. On his return from exile in 1660 he was created President of the Council and three years later became Lord High Commissioner. The Duke of Lauderdale, whose ruthless and unpleasant character is so clearly conveyed by Lely [fig. 1], held the most powerful office as Secretary of State for Scotland, and was, under the King, the effective ruler of the country.

David Paton, one of the finest Scottish artists of the seventeenth century, had close ties with the Maitland family. He accompanied the Duchess of Lauderdale's son on his grand tour, visiting the court of Cosimo III de'Medici in Florence. Paton occasionally painted in oil, for instance the portrait of General Tam Dalyell at The Binns. But he is better-known now, as he was in his lifetime, for his miniatures drawn in plumbago (graphite), or sometimes in ink. His skills obviously impressed the Florentine court as much as they did his fellow countrymen. Giraldi, the Tuscan ambassador in London, preferred his earlier work to his later, admiring its force and directness, perhaps having a work like the Yester Lords in mind [*12*]. Paton's portrait of John Graham of Claverhouse, the famous Jacobite leader known as 'Bonnie Dundee', who was killed at the battle of Killiecrankie, cannot date from much later than 1670, given the apparent youth of the sitter [*13*].

Dundee and Dalyell were the type of ruthless, professional soldier that Lauderdale used to suppress the covenanters. They were his instruments for reimposing episcopal government in the Church. But there was another aspect of Lauderdale's policy of restoring the King's authority in Scotland which had a wholly beneficial effect. This was the transformation of Holyroodhouse from an overgrown and old-fashioned tower house into a magnificent baroque palace, intended to be an expression in stone of the King's power and presence in Scotland.

The architect was Sir William Bruce, whose portrait Wright painted in 1664 [*14*]. As Surveyor of the Royal Works he also had the responsibility for finding plasterers, sculptors and painters. The sculptor Jan van Santvoort and the painter Jacob de Wet were brought over from Holland to take part in Scotland's greatest artistic project of the century. Both painter and sculptor combined work at the palace with commissions in the country, notably at Glamis, where the Earl of Strathmore had de Wet paint his chapel and Santvoort carve the royal arms and his own

13
DAVID PATON
John Graham of Claverhouse,
Viscount Dundee (*c.* 1649–89)

Ink on paper
4⅛ x 3¼ (10.5 x 8.3)
Scottish National Portrait Gallery

A distinguished soldier whose services were used by the Crown to suppress militant covenanters at Bothwell Bridge and elsewhere, Dundee died for the recently exiled King James VII at Killiecrankie. Paton's fine portrait explains why the man who was reviled by the covenanters as 'Bloody Clavers' was known to his supporters as 'Bonnie Dundee'.

14
JOHN MICHAEL WRIGHT
Sir William Bruce (*c.* 1630–1710)

Signed and dated: 166? (almost certainly 1664)
Oil on canvas
28½ x 24 (72.4 x 61.0)
Scottish National Portrait Gallery

Bruce played a not inconsiderable political role before 1671, when he was appointed the King's Surveyor and Master of Works. In that capacity his great project was the transformation of Holyroodhouse into a baroque palace for the King. He was the architect of his own house at Kinross and was much consulted in architectural as well as horticultural matters, on which he was also an expert.

Fig. 2
The Apotheosis of Hercules by Jacob de Wet. The Palace of Holyroodhouse. Reproduced by Gracious Permission of Her Majesty The Queen

bust over the front door of the castle. At Balcaskie and Kinross, both houses built and owned by Sir William Bruce, artists and craftsmen were seconded from the palace. Had the Holyrood project not existed, then the baroque style in Scotland would have been much less widespread, limited to a handful of ducal seats like Thirlestane and Drumlanrig whose owners were rich enough to import their own craftsmen. The number of foreign artists working in Scotland increased with the century. Some, like Vorstermans, whose view of Stirling Castle may have been a royal commission, appear to have stayed only briefly. Others, like Schunemann, patronised by the Earl of Wemyss and the Duke of Rothes, or John Slezer, stayed many years. Slezer was a military engineer and surveyor. He was brought from Holland to work on the Holyrood project and by 1677 was acting as building supervisor to the Duke of Lauderdale. He is remembered today for his engraved topographical views of the great houses and towns of Scotland, published as the *Theatrum Scotiae*.

Jacob de Wet arrived in Scotland in 1673 to take up a key role in the refurbishment of Holyroodhouse. He was the chief painter, brought over from Holland because there was no resident artist able to paint the mythological and

15
JACOB DE WET
The Triumph of Galatea
Oil on canvas
23½ x 28 (59.7 x 71.1)
Private collection, Ireland

Painted in about 1675, this is the only known oil sketch for any of de Wet's work at Holyroodhouse. The finished painting, in the King's antechamber, shows only the central part of the composition.

allegorical scenes that the new style of decoration demanded. On the ceiling of the King's bedchamber, de Wet, alluding to the King himself, painted the Apotheosis of Hercules [fig. 2] and, in the Privy Chamber, Cupid and Psyche. He painted the Triumph of Galatea [15] in the King's antechamber, and in the King's closet the subject of the Finding of Moses was chosen because of the legend that the royal family were descended from Scota, pharaoh's daughter.

De Wet appears to have travelled back and forth across the North Sea between Scotland and Europe. He became a member of the Painters' Corporation of Cologne in 1677 and in 1688 he again left his house in the Canongate for a year or so away. His wife Helena was granted authority to collect the money that was owing for work he had completed.

On 26 February 1684 de Wet signed a contract for another royal commission, painting the portraits of Charles II and all the previous 110 Scottish kings. He had two years to complete the set, an annual salary of £120, and a clause in his agreement which prevented him from accepting other work. De Wet was able to base some of his portraits on those which George Jamesone, half a century earlier, had painted for the ceremonial entry into Edinburgh of Charles I. Jamesone's kings had been set into a triumphal arch in the High Street. De Wet's were commissioned for the Long Gallery of Holyroodhouse, where they can still be seen, darkened with age and made cruder through three centuries of cleaning and repainting. They were never great works of art, nor were they

16

JACOB DE WET

Still-life with a Skull

Signed: De Witt pinx^t
Oil on canvas
29 $\frac{1}{5}$ x 24 $\frac{2}{5}$ (74.2 x 62.0)
The Rt Honble the Earl of
Seafield

This is the only still-life by de Wet known to survive. It is likely, however, to be one of several that he painted in Scotland.

intended to be. Probably hung in chronological order, they were painted to illustrate the King's Scottish ancestry, with its origins in the mythic past. Almost as important as the painted image was the name of the king which De Wet was contracted to inscribe on each canvas, smaller letters for the lesser-known, like Mogaldus and Euthodius II, capital letters for the more important, offering a condensed history of the Scottish royal family from Fergus to Charles.

De Wet's other main commission in Scotland was his work for the Earl of Strathmore at Glamis, where he decorated the chapel and painted ceilings and pictures of Icarus, Diana and Europa as well as portraits of the family. His commission to paint the dining-room ceiling stipulated that the subject should be 'The full historie of some one or other of Ovid's Metamorphosis . . . designed by Mr De Vite and expected by the said Earle that the same shall be well done as that it may be of credit to the one and satisfactione to the other.'[2] He was assisted by William Rennie, a Dundee painter, who had worked for the Earl on his own behalf at Castle Lyon (Huntly Castle) and Longforgan Church. Lord Strathmore complained

that de Wet had overcharged him, and he resented the fact that Rennie had undertaken parts of the decoration which had been specifically contracted to the senior artist.

De Wet carried out work for many Scottish families [16], among them the Makgills of Cousland and the Clerks of Penicuik [17]. One of his finest portraits is the full-length of John, 1st Marquis of Atholl [fig. 3], the hammer of the covenanters at the battle of Pentland Hills and a leader of the 'Highland Host' against the Campbells in the west. De Wet depicted the Marquis as a military hero with an allusion to Achilles, since the bas-relief behind him shows Thetis and Cupid in Vulcan's forge. The battle of Bothwell Bridge, where Atholl played a major part in the defeat of the covenanters, is shown on the right of the canvas. There de Wet may have been inspired by Rubens's oil sketch of the Capture of Paris by Henri IV.

The Marquis's wife, Lady Amelia Stanley, was painted by John Michael Wright, as was their son Mungo [18]. Little is known of him apart from a notice or two in the family chronicle, as, for instance, in 1697, where he is recorded as pursuing Simon Fraser, Lord Lovat, marching 'in a belted plad to admiration which did encourage the men much.'[3] Wright's portrait shows Lord Mungo dressed for hunting rather than fighting. Earlier in the century a visiting

17
JACOB DE WET
The Highland Wedding
Oil on canvas
37 x 51 (94.0 x 129.5)
Sir John Clerk of Penicuik, Bt

First recorded at Penicuik in 1724, this painting, together with family portraits by de Wet, was probably commissioned by Sir John Clerk [5]. It is based on Dutch prototypes – for instance the kermesses of Teniers – but the scene is made distinctively Scottish by the landscape, the architecture and the costume of the piper. A version, possibly later in date, is owned by the National Museums of Scotland.

27

Fig. 3
John Murray, Marquis of Atholl, by Jacob de Wet. His Grace the Duke of Atholl

Englishman had described a Highland hunt he had attended: 'For once in the yeere, which is the whole moneth of August, and sometimes part of September, many of the nobility and gentry of the Kingdome (for their pleasure) doe come into these Highland countries to hunt, where they doe conforme themselves to the habite of the Highland men, who, for the moste part, speake nothing but Irish [Gaelic] . . . Their habite is shooes with but one sole apiece; stockings (which they call short hose) made of a warme stuff of divers colours, which they call tartane. As for breeches, many of them, nor their forefathers, never wore any, but a jerkin of the same stuffe that their hose is of, their garters being bands or wreathes of hay or straw, with a plaed about their shoulders, which is a mantle of divers colours, much finer and lighter stuffe than their hose, with blue flat caps on their heads, a handkerchiefe knit with two knots about their necke; and thus are they attyred. Now, their weapons are long bowes and forked arrowes, swords and targets, harquebusses, muskets, durks, and Loquhabor-axes. With these arms I found many of them armed for the hunting. As for their attire,

18
JOHN MICHAEL WRIGHT
Lord Mungo Murray (1668–1700)
Oil on canvas
88½ x 60¾ (224.8 x 154.3)
Scottish National Portrait Gallery

The identity of the sitter has only recently been discovered to be Mungo Murray, the fifth son of the Marquis of Atholl. Wright appears to have painted the portrait in Ireland in the early 1680s. The sitter died young fighting the Spanish in Panama during the last days of the ill-fated Scottish colony of Darien.

any man of what degree soever that comes amongst them, must not disdaine to weare it; for if they doe, then they will disdaine to hunt, or willingly to bring in their dogges; but if men be kind unto them, and be in their habit, then they are conquered with kindnesse, and the sport will be plentifull. This was the reason that I found so many noblemen and gentlemen in those shapes.'[4]

Through his mother's relatives, the Earls of Derby, Mungo Murray could claim kinship with the Irish Dukes of Ormonde, a family like the Atholls of strong Royalist sympathies. Two versions of Wright's portrait were in the Ormonde collection in the seventeenth century. One as early as 1684, when Mungo was only sixteen, is listed in an inventory at Kilkenny Castle. A second portrait was at Ormonde House in London in 1689.

Wright was in Ireland for the four years between 1679 and 1683, a period of Roman Catholic persecution in London. In 1680 he painted the full-length portrait of Sir Neil O'Neil in Irish dress, a version of which also found its way into the Ormonde collection. It seems most likely that Lord Mungo, in common with other Highland noblemen's

19

JOHN MICHAEL WRIGHT

King James VII, as Duke of York
(1633–1701)

Oil on canvas
44½ x 39 (113.0 x 99.1)
Government Art Collection

The portrait was painted in the early 1660s, shortly after the Restoration. Wright portrayed the Duke standing as a soldier in front of a campaign tent; he had indeed fought bravely in France in the 1650s. Around the coat of arms, roses and thistles are entwined symbolising England and Scotland, which were then united only by a common monarchy.

sons, was in Ireland as part of his education, attached to the court of a distinguished and politically sympathetic Irish family to which he himself was connected. The portrait was probably painted in Ireland, commissioned by the Duke of Ormonde as a distinctive Scottish image and a pair to the very Irish portrait of Sir Neil O'Neil.

Another portrait by Wright which may also have been painted as an illustration of national character is the large triple portrait of the actor John Lacy, painted for Charles II. Lacy appears to be dressed as a Scot (in Highland costume), a Frenchman and an Englishman. So popular was this portrait that there were two versions of it in the same sale in Edinburgh in 1697.

At the same time that John Michael Wright had prudently crossed to Ireland to avoid anti-Catholic persecution in England, the King's brother, James, Duke of York, also a Roman Catholic, had been hurried out of the capital [*19*]. He was given the Duke of Lauderdale's former post of High Commissioner and a seat on the powerful Privy Council. He and his wife, Maria d'Este, Mary of Modena, took occupation of the newly refurbished Palace of Holyroodhouse. The couple arrived in Edinburgh in 1679, and for the first time in living memory the capital was host to a royal court. During the three years James spent in Edinburgh, and later, as a consequence of his interest in the city, there was a flowering of

Fig. 4
The Chapel Royal, Holyroodhouse. Engraving by Mazell after Wyck from Vitruvius Scoticus. Reproduced by permission of the Royal Commission on the Ancient and Historical Monuments of Scotland

artistic and cultural life. The city and the university both received new charters, the Royal College of Physicians was established, the Advocates' Library was founded, the Order of the Thistle instituted, the new Physic Garden was encouraged, and there was theatre at Holyrood. The Abbey Church was transformed into the Chapel Royal for the use of the new Order of the Thistle and adapted for the Roman Mass [fig. 4]. James Smith, Bruce's successor as Surveyor of the Royal Works, was the architect, and the wood carvers were William Morgan and Grinling Gibbons. Communion silver, candlesticks and vestments were ordered from Edinburgh, London and the Continent.

In 1685, on the death of his brother, the Duke of York ascended the throne as King James VII and II. One of his first political initiatives was an embassy to Pope Innocent XI, led by Lord Castlemaine, with John Michael Wright as artistic director. His role was to organise the very elaborate ceremonial and display which formed the setting for the political negotiations. But James's politics were less successful than Wright's art, and the Pope, alarmed at the King's haste in restoring Catholic rights in Britain, accurately predicted the Protestant backlash that forced James from his throne at the end of 1688.

It was not only James whose world had collapsed. Wright too never recovered. 'For his royal master being now gone, he soon found that he had lost an extraordinary friend, and 'tis therefore from that time that he dated his own ruin.'[5] In December 1688 the Chapel Royal was sacked by a Protestant mob, its new fittings destroyed, its silver stolen. The brief renaissance of the palace was over.

31

Sir John de Medina, William Gouw Ferguson, John Scougal and the patronage of the Earls of Leven and Melville

'Sir John Medina Painter, born at Brussells in the year 1659 (of a good family his father coll of a Regiment.) He learnt of Du Chattell portrait painter. Marry'd young afterwards came to England in year 1686 . . . staide here several years painted many portraits of eminent persons, amongst which were many Scotch Noblemen. The Earl of Leven his grand patron got him the encouragement of 500 pounds subscription to goe to Scotland where he went to paint portraits. Painted most of the Quality of Scotland.'[6]
Thus the London diarist George Vertue summarised Medina's career. In his brief account he mentioned, as well he might, the role of David, 3rd Earl of Leven, in bringing the artist to Scotland. Even a near contemporary like Vertue, though, can have had little idea of the effort and persistence of the Earl and his family in persuading the artist to leave his Drury Lane studio for the uncertain prospect of a career in Edinburgh.

Lined up against the reluctant artist [20] were three determined women, Lord Leven's wife Anna, his mother Catherine, Countess of Melville, and Catherine's first cousin Margaret, Countess of Rothes. They felt that there was no artist talented enough in Scotland in the 1690s to paint them or their children. Their husbands could be painted in London by Sir Godfrey Kneller, but as they were unlikely to travel south more than once or twice in their lifetimes they were obliged to submit themselves to the inferior talents of the Scougal family.

While David Scougal was alive this was bearable, but even so Lady Rothes must have been all too aware that while her father had been glamorised by Wright in London [11], her mother's homely features had been unflatteringly recorded by David Scougal in Scotland [6].

33

20
SIR JOHN DE MEDINA
Self-portrait
Oil on canvas
30⅜ x 25 (77.2 x 63.5)
Scottish National Portrait Gallery

Three self-portraits by Medina are known: this, of c. 1700; the portrait of 1708, which was painted at the request of the surgeons of Edinburgh and which still hangs with their portraits at Surgeons' Hall; and a portrait of unknown date, possibly the earliest of the three, which Alexander, 2nd Duke of Gordon, presented to Cosimo III de'Medici. It is now in the Uffizi Gallery, Florence.

After David Scougal's death in about 1680, the best portrait painter resident in Scotland was John Scougal, probably the son or nephew of David, but not his equal as an artist. For Lord Leven and his relations, Scottish portraiture had sunk below an acceptable level, and a better, more sophisticated painter was needed. In 1691 they found their man.

In that year the Earl of Leven, his father George, 1st Earl of Melville, and his mother, the Countess of Melville, sat to Medina in London [21, 22, 23]. Both father and son had been political exiles during the last years of the reign of James VII; Melville, implicated in the Rye House Plot of 1683, fled with his son to Holland, where they then joined the court of Prince William of Orange. Lord Leven was employed by William to negotiate German support for his invasion of England, and when that took place in 1688 both father and son were closely involved. Lord Leven, with a regiment he had raised abroad, was put in charge of Plymouth, the first city to fall to the House of Orange.

Back in Scotland Lord Melville was one of the leaders of the party in Parliament keen to proclaim William and Mary King and Queen of Scotland. In May 1689 he was

21

SIR JOHN DE MEDINA

George, 1st Earl of Melville
(1636–1707)

Oil on canvas
50 x 40⅛ (127.0 x 101.9)
Scottish National Portrait Gallery

This, one of Medina's finest male portraits, is of a man who was one of King William's principal supporters in Scotland. A version of this portrait, of equally high quality and also painted in 1691, remains in family ownership.

22

SIR JOHN DE MEDINA

Catherine, Countess of Melville
(died 1713)

Oil on canvas
50 x 40 (127.0 x 101.7)
The Rt Honble the Earl of Leven
and Melville

The wife of George, 1st Earl of Melville, Catherine Leslie was the daughter of Alexander, 1st Earl of Leven. After the death of her brother, the 2nd Earl, and his two daughters, the Leven earldom passed to her son David.

35

Fig. 5
*Archibald, 1st Duke of Argyll, with his
sons John (later 2nd Duke) and Archibald (later 3rd Duke), by Sir John de
Medina. His Grace the Duke of Argyll*

rewarded by being created sole Secretary of State. The
earldom was granted in the following year, an acknow-
ledgement of Melville's position as one of the leading
supporters of the new regime in a country where many still
remained loyal to the House of Stewart.

Whether Lord Melville and his son met Medina abroad is
not known. The artist was in Brussels until 1686, when he
moved to London, setting himself up as a rival to Kneller,
whose prices he was, without difficulty, able to undercut.
Archibald, 10th Earl of Argyll, was an early patron, sitting
to Medina with his two sons in about 1689 [fig. 5]. Like
Lord Leven, the Earl had joined Prince William's invasion and, for his continued and very valuable support for

23
SIR JOHN DE MEDINA

David, 3rd Earl of Leven, 2nd Earl of Melville (1660–1728)

Signed and dated: J B Medina fecit 1691

Oil on canvas

50 x 40 (127.0 x 101.7)

Scottish National Portrait Gallery

Lord Leven was Medina's chief patron and the man instrumental in bringing him to Scotland. They were indebted to each other, Lord Leven owing Medina money at the time of his death.

the new regime, was created 1st Duke of Argyll in 1701. The imposing and richly coloured portrait of Argyll and his children shows that in Medina Kneller now had a rival whose abilities were not to be underestimated.

Medina and Kneller were two of a large number of artists and craftsmen born and trained in Northern Europe who settled in London after the Restoration and profited from the renaissance of the arts under Charles II and his brother James. Grinling Gibbons, whom Medina drew, had arrived from Rotterdam at the beginning of the 1670s. The portrait painter John Closterman had settled in London in 1681. During the 1680s a further flood of Protestant craftsmen arrived in London when the Huguenots were persecuted and then expelled from France. While England had earlier produced native painters of distinction, the last two decades of the seventeenth century were a time when foreigners, and foreign portrait painters in particular, dominated the London scene. Medina was comfortable in this milieu and had no wish to uproot his wife and young family. But Lord Leven persisted, pleased presumably with the portraits of himself and his parents, and prompted by his female relations. An offer was made, negotiations continued, the offer was improved. At last, in September 1693, a bargain was struck.

'Medina intends to come to Scotland with my Lord upon these conditions, that there is a probability that he will get 20 half lengths to doe or 40 three quarters and £10 for the on[e] and 5 for the other besides the frames . . . This is no price in comparison of Kneller for he takes £24 and £12. I wish you would give yourself the trouble to show My Lady Rothes (who desired me to doe what I could to persuade him to come to Scotland) that he is coming and she and you may make a guess what number of pictures may be taken from him by your relations, and of what sizes, that he may both see if it be worth his while to goe, and make provisions according to his work. He is only to stay so long as to doe all the faces of his pictures and is to bring them here with him to finish them . . . If you can condescend upon the persons to be drawn, the size and the garb, a good many may be so blocked as that he'll finish them before he goes.'[7]

Some time either at the end of 1693 or the beginning of the following year Medina travelled north to paint the heads on his already completed bodies. Among the first to attend his studio must have been members of the Earl of Leven's immediate family and their friends, the men and women who had notified Lady Leven in advance. The Countess of Rothes, for instance, whose head sits none too happily on her shoulders, was painted in 1694 [24]. Medina based his composition on a pose published in a mezzotint of Sophia Carolina, the Electress of Hanover, and the only part of the portrait which was certainly painted in Scotland is the Countess's head.

Medina did not intend to stay long, but during 1694 he was busy and successful and he would have realised that there was no serious competition in Scotland. Lord Leven's assurances to him of business were fulfilled and so he sent for his wife and children, his furniture and studio equipment and installed them in a house in the Canongate.

Already he had gained the favour of several of the leading families of Scotland and through them came other commissions. The Countess of Leven was born Lady Anna Wemyss, and it was no doubt through her recommendation that Medina received the orders from the Wemyss family for five whole-length portraits and one half-length during his first year in Scotland. When Lady Anna's brother, Lord Elcho, returned from the south two years later, Medina was again the artist chosen to paint him. Many of Lady Rothes's relations were painted, including

24
SIR JOHN DE MEDINA
Margaret, Countess of Rothes
(c. 1660–1700)

Signed and dated: J B Medina P
1694
Oil on canvas
49 x 39½ (124.5 x 100.3)
The Rt Honble the Earl of
Haddington

*Medina's composition is taken in reverse
from Schenck's mezzotint portrait of the
Electress of Hanover. The Electress had
earlier used her influence on behalf of the
Countess's relations to obtain a position
for the Earl of Leven in the service of her
son-in-law, the Elector of Brandenburg.*

her two sons, the Earl of Rothes and the Earl of Haddington, her sisters-in-law and their children. In a society where kinship was important and family connections amongst the nobility very close, patronage by one family led quickly to further contacts and employment.

The aristocracy still lived for much of the year in the closes and lands off the High Street. While Medina rapidly became their painter he was also patronised by Edinburgh's increasingly large professional middle class, the lawyers, clerics and merchants of the city. At the Royal College of Surgeons there can still be seen Medina's set of oval portraits of the members of the old Incorporation of Surgeons, mostly painted in the last decade of the artist's life. The first portraits of the series appear to date from about 1697, when James Smith's new Surgeons' Hall was opened. Quite why some members were painted and others were not is unknown – perhaps it was because they paid for their portraits themselves. Medina's set is unique. No other contemporary series of portraits of members of a professional society is known to have existed, and only Kneller's portraits of the members of London's Kit-cat

25
SIR JOHN DE MEDINA
Apelles and Campaspe
Oil on canvas
49½ x 49½ (125.7 x 125.7)
The Rt Honble the Earl of
Wemyss and March, K.T.

Alexander the Great commissioned his favourite painter Apelles to paint his mistress Campaspe. While the artist worked and Cupid, the god of love, ground his colours, Apelles fell in love himself. In an act of celebrated generosity Alexander relinquished his mistress to Apelles. [Reproduced in colour on the front cover.]

Club are comparable. Slightly smaller than the Kit-cat portraits, Medina's are more loosely painted. During the last decade of his life the artist drew more and more with his brush, expressing shape and contour graphically rather than through colour. At its best, Medina's later, freer style is most successful in conveying quite subtle differences of character while at the same time offering a satisfying surface of rhythm and texture.

Although portraiture was his speciality there must have been a market for Medina's accomplished figure paintings, of which Apelles and Campaspe [25] is the largest and best. They show the good effects of his Flemish studio training in the liveliness and assuredness of his drawing. Cain and Abel [26] was copied from a plaster, which he owned, after an original by the Flemish sculptor Giambologna. The model for Pallas Athene [27] may have been drawn from the life in Medina's Canongate studio.

Medina lived in Scotland for nearly twenty years, his style keeping abreast of fashion in London. The full, sonorous baroque portraits of the 1690s give way to the lighter, freer, less formal portraits of the following decade. Sometimes, though, his later work can be slipshod. His studio must have been a busy place, and pressure on him and his assistants to produce was great. At his best – and the portraits of his own children [28] are some of his finest

26

SIR JOHN DE MEDINA

Cain and Abel

Oil on canvas

29 x 23 (73.7 x 58.4)

Sir John Clerk of Penicuik, Bt

One of the items listed in Medina's collection at the time of his death was a plaster-of-paris group of Cain and Abel. This is likely to have been the model from which [26] was painted. The plaster was a small reproduction of Giambologna's famous marble sculpture of Samson and the Philistine, which, when Medina was living in London, could be seen in the garden of York House, where it was believed to represent Cain and Abel.

27

SIR JOHN DE MEDINA

Pallas Athene

Oil on canvas

30 x 25 (76.2 x 63.5)

Sir John Clerk of Penicuik, Bt

The Greek goddess Pallas Athene, the daughter of Zeus, is shown with her attribute, the Gorgon-faced shield. The high quality of this picture, carefully drawn and fluently painted, is typical of the artist's figure paintings.

28
SIR JOHN DE MEDINA
John Medina (before 1686–1764)
Oil on canvas
30¼ x 25 (77.0 x 63.5)
National Gallery of Scotland

The portrait probably shows the artist's son John, who later became a painter.

paintings – Medina was a very talented and distinctive artist, working at a time when individuality was not a noticeable characteristic of British art.

While Medina was a foreign artist who saw an opening and settled in Scotland, there were a number of Scots artists in the second half of the seventeenth century who went in the other direction. Some, like Thomas Murray, made London their destination, but many others travelled further afield. James Hamilton was born in Lanarkshire about ten years before Medina and spent his career as a painter of still-lifes in Germany and the Low Countries. He died in Brussels, the city of Medina's birth, in about 1720. Just as Medina's painter son and grandson are part of the history of Scottish art in the eighteenth century, so Hamilton's three sons, with their Christian names of Ferdinand Phillipp, Johann Georg and Karl Wilhelm, fit comfortably into the history of German art.

Jan Collison and John Cruden from Aberdeen both worked further east. Collison was made Polish court painter in Warsaw in 1664, while John Cruden worked in Silesia. He was assistant to Claude Callot from 1667 until the Frenchman's death in 1687. In 1691 he became court painter to the Bishop of Wrocław.

29
WILLIAM GOUW FERGUSON
Still-life and Dead Game
Signed and dated: W G F fe A°
1677
Oil on canvas
59 x 49 (149.9 x 121.9)
National Gallery of Scotland

This is the most elaborate of all Ferguson's still-lifes. It is very similar to work by contemporary Dutch artists with whom he worked.

William Gouw Ferguson, like James Hamilton, was also a specialist in still-life, and both artists must have realised that the market for their work was too small in Scotland. Ferguson was living in The Hague in the 1660s. He travelled in France and Italy but in 1681 was back in the Netherlands, living in Amsterdam, the centre of the European art trade. This was important for an artist who specialised in a field other than portraiture and who needed to make use of the large, efficient international art market which the city provided.

The continuing presence of so many of Ferguson's works in old Scottish collections suggests that he kept in contact with his native country. His only recorded commission was indeed for a Scottish family: an overmantel, in which he depicted a sorceress charming a serpent, and an over-door of a sarcophagus and urns which were painted in about 1673 for the Duchess of Lauderdale's private closet at Ham House, where they still remain. These two paintings are examples of a type which Vertue described as 'of Basso Rilievos, antique, Stones. Very carefully and well painted the light thrown into ye pictures very surprisingly. These done by *Ferguson* a Scott when in Italy.'

43

30
WILLIAM GOUW FERGUSON

Landscape with Women Washing
by an Antique Tomb

Oil on canvas
$27\frac{1}{2}$ x 39 (69.8 x 99.0)
Private collection

*Ferguson mostly painted still-lifes but he
also produced a number of pictures showing ruined classical monuments and bas-
reliefs. They were admired in his day,
and this one, which appears to show a
monument to Bacchus, is a particularly
fine example.*

Fig. 6
*A flower-piece by William Gouw
Ferguson. Museum Flehite, Amersfoort*

31
WILLIAM GOUW FERGUSON
Still-life with Dead Birds
Signed and dated: W G Ferguson
Fecit A 1662
Oil on canvas
19½ x 25½ (49.5 x 64.8)
Dundee Art Gallery and Museums

Apart from a single flower-piece [fig. 6], most of Ferguson's work consists of detailed still-lifes with dead game birds. The largest of these [29], his masterpiece, is entirely Dutch in style, very close in fact to the work of his contemporaries and competitors Jan Weenix and Willem van Aelst. It seems he must have trained as well as lived in Holland.

Ferguson had two possible methods of selling his work. One was to paint on commission for a family like the Lauderdales, the other was to produce small-scale works specifically for auction. In 1693 a sale was held in the Lawnmarket in Edinburgh, opposite Gladstone's Land, where no fewer than eight of his pictures were up for sale. So unvarying is his work that no individual item can now be identified from the catalogue entries. Several of the lots, like 212, 'A pidgeon and small birds finelly painted by Ferguson', or 258, 'A Curious piece of Ruins by Ferguson', could describe two of the paintings illustrated here [30, 31].

John Scougal lived further down the High Street, opposite St Giles, on the east side of Advocates' Close. There he had his house, studio, and apparently a gallery where his paintings could be seen. The arrival of Medina in the city where he was already an established artist must have been a set-back for Scougal; but in Edinburgh, as in

45

32

JOHN SCOUGAL

William Aikman (1646–99)

Oil on canvas
30 x 25 (76.2 x 63.5)
Lt Col. Sir John Inglefield-
Watson, Bt

William Aikman of Cairnie, the father of the painter William Aikman [40], was Clerk of the Faculty of Advocates and Sheriff Depute of Angus. The portrait, probably painted in the early 1680s, is likely to be an early work of John Scougal.

London, more people were having their portraits painted at the end of the seventeenth century than ever before. There was enough work for both artists to prosper.

John Scougal's early work shows the influence of David Scougal, with whom it is almost certain he trained and worked. There is a scarcity of documented paintings from the beginning of his career, but it seems quite possible that a group of portraits formerly attributed to an anonymous artist called the 'Lanark Painter' may be early works of his. The portraits of William and Margaret Aikman [32, 33] are two such paintings; they probably date from the early 1680s. A portrait like John Birnie of Broomhill [fig. 7] of 1693 links these early portraits with a group of securely documented works of the early eighteenth century, for instance the pair of portraits of Sir Francis and Lady Grant, for which the bill of 1700 survives [34,35]. From the portraits of the Aikmans, through John Birnie, to the Grants, there is a coherent stylistic development, one of progressive simplification. In fact John Scougal's style became increasingly perfunctory as he grew older, and some of his last portraits, of the early years of the eighteenth century, seem almost to have been assembled

33
JOHN SCOUGAL

Margaret Aikman (married 1674)

Oil on canvas
30 x 25 (76.2 x 63.5)
Lt Col. Sir John Inglefield-
Watson, Bt

*The sitter was the wife of William Aik-
man [32], the mother of the painter, and
the sister of Sir John Clerk of Penicuik
[5].*

Fig. 7
*John Birnie of Broomhill, by John Scou-
gal. Private collection*

47

34
JOHN SCOUGAL

Sir Francis Grant, Lord Cullen
(1658–1726)

Oil on canvas
30 x 25½ (76.2 x 64.8)
Sir Archibald Grant of Monymusk,
Bt

In September 1700 John Scougal was paid six guineas and a groat for this and the companion portrait of Lady Grant [35]. Sir Francis's portrait of c. 1720 by Smibert is [54] below.

35
JOHN SCOUGAL

Jane Meldrum, Lady Grant
(dates not known)

Oil on canvas
30 x 25½ (76.2 x 64.8)
Sir Archibald Grant of Monymusk,
Bt

As Lady Grant had died by the time Smibert painted the large family group of the Grants of Monymusk [54], this portrait was shown in the picture hanging behind Lord Cullen.

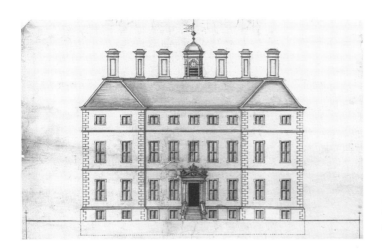

Fig. 8
Melville House, Fife, drawn by its architect James Smith. Reproduced by permission of the Scottish Record Office (RHP 4093)

from kits, with almond-shaped eyes a particular speciality. It would be wrong to think that Medina was the painter of the aristocracy and John Scougal of the middle classes. The Wemyss family, for instance, employed Scougal before Medina's arrival and continued to use him subsequently. So did the Baillies at Mellerstain, but Medina was the more fashionable artist and might not have attempted some of the jobs that fell to John Scougal, like the copies he painted of royal portraits for Glasgow Town Council.

John Scougal died a very old man in 1737, but he appears to have given up painting in 1715. By then he was rich, with property in Edinburgh and lucrative salmon fishing on the Don near Aberdeen, where his wife, and very likely his own family, originated.

Medina's career was even more successful. He was naturalised a Scot and was knighted in 1707; when he died three years later his estate was valued at more than £14,000 Scots. Medina's association with the Earls of Leven and Melville continued throughout his life. He painted at least fifteen portraits of Lord Leven, most of them for relations or political colleagues. One or two would certainly have been hung at Melville House in Fife, the grand new family seat built between 1697 and 1703 by James Smith to replace Monimail House [fig. 8]. There they would have had the setting they deserved: although the outside is classical and austere, the interior was once richly and lavishly decorated. The greatest piece of furniture to survive from the original plenishings is the magnificent seventeenth-century State Bed [fig. 9], still hung with its original crimson silk Genoa velvets and white Chinese silk damasks. The house, the bed and Medina's portraits were assembled to create an effect of sumptuous magnificence with the purpose of impressing the visitor with the wealth and political importance of the family.

Fig. 9
The State Bed from Melville House. Reproduced by permission of the Trustees of the Victoria and Albert Museum, London

49

Argyll

William Aikman, James Norie and the patronage of John, 2nd Duke of Argyll

'His Grace of Argyll', wrote the painter William Aikman from London in 1724, 'is as much my friend as ever and every day I have some mark of it or other so that I'm happy enough here in good Padrons and cannot fail of success if the want of it proceeds not from my own weakness.'[8]

Aikman's patron was the great statesman and soldier John, 2nd Duke of Argyll and 1st Duke of Greenwich, a hero of the Duke of Marlborough's campaigns in Flanders, the pre-eminent Scottish politician of his age and the head of Clan Campbell [36]. It was the Duke's advice to the painter to move south from Edinburgh and it was the Duke's patronage which supported him on his arrival.

The two men were almost exact contemporaries, coming to manhood and inheritance at the beginning of the reign of Queen Anne. But whereas William Aikman was the son of an Angus laird [32] and a graduate of the University of Edinburgh, the Duke was the chief of one of the greatest Scottish clans, able to raise an army of five thousand men. His rent-paying lands covered five hundred square miles in Argyll, and he held feudal superiority over a further three thousand square miles. For much of the seventeenth century the Presbyterian Campbells had been at variance with the royal family; the Duke's grand- and great-grandfather [2] had both been executed; but with the flight of the Roman Catholic King James VII and the accession of the Protestant Prince William of Orange, the Argylls were back in favour. Medina's portrait of Archibald, 10th Earl, and his two sons John and Archibald was painted shortly after the Earl had landed in England with William [fig. 5, page 36]. The earldom was raised to a dukedom in 1701, and as John, the eldest son, never had a male heir, Medina's portrait shows the first three Dukes of Argyll. It was painted in London, where at Ham House, home of their grandmother, the Duchess of Lauderdale, John and his younger brother were born and brought up. A few

36
WILLIAM AIKMAN

John, 2nd Duke of Argyll and
Duke of Greenwich (1678–1743)

Oil on canvas
95 x 59 (241.3 x 150.0)
By Gracious Permission of Her
Majesty The Queen

*The date of this portrait is not known, but
it appears to be contemporary with Kneller's full-length of 1717 (Drumlanrig).
The military setting could allude to one of
several episodes in the Duke's distinguished career, as lieutenant-general
under Marlborough in Flanders, as
ambassador and commander-in-chief in
Spain, or as commander-in-chief against
the Jacobite army at the battle of
Sheriffmuir.*

years later Medina moved his studio north to Edinburgh,
where he remained for the rest of his life. It was there that
Aikman received his first instructions as an artist.

Initially, as a second son, Aikman had planned a career for
himself in business. His cousins ran a well-established
import-export business at Leghorn servicing Anglo-
Italian trade. To this end he made progress in civil law at
the university, but the deaths of his elder brother and
father left him, as a very young man, laird of his family
estate at Cairnie, on the edge of Arbroath, and under
pressure from his mother's family, the Clerks of Penicuik
[5, 7], to read for the bar instead. For whatever reason,
Aikman became neither a lawyer nor a merchant, but after

a decade of study and travel he emerged as the leading Scottish painter of his generation.

Although Aikman did not serve an apprenticeship to Medina, he learnt the rudiments of his craft from him, and his few surviving, or rather identified, early portraits show the older artist's strong stylistic influence. After a year or two in Edinburgh, Aikman went to London to continue his training. He learnt drawing, anatomy and architecture, bought prints, medals and paintings as aids for his studies, and spent time copying portraits at Kensington Palace. He began to get commissions, and a man who was particularly useful in this respect was Dr John Arbuthnott, the friend of Pope and Swift, whose own birthplace and family were only some twenty-five miles away from Aikman's, in the Mearns.

Aikman was conscious of his initial success in London and he wrote to his uncle in 1705 that he stood a good chance of painting Queen Anne and her consort Prince George. But he harboured an ambition to visit Italy, and Rome in particular, where, at the centre of the two worlds of ancient and modern art, he could complete his studies. To travel so far and to live independently with a servant for several years was expensive, so he sold his estate in Angus and other property he owned in New Jersey and planned to travel out to Venice with the Earl of Manchester's embassy. Unfortunately his money did not come through in time and he was still in London on 1 May 1707, when, in his own words, 'The Queen this day touchd the Act [of Union] so we are no more Scots and English but all bold Brittains.'[9]

While there was mixed feeling in Scotland about union with England – there was rioting in the streets of Glasgow and Edinburgh – Aikman and his relations are likely to have been in favour. Sir John Clerk, the painter's cousin, was one of the first of the new Barons of the Exchequer and he owed this position to his patron, the Duke of Queensberry, a prominent unionist. The Duke of Argyll, as Lord High Commissioner to the Scottish Parliament, had also been active in promoting the Union as a means of ensuring the Protestant succession and to ease the country's considerable economic problems. For his efforts he was created Baron Chatham and Earl of Greenwich, enabling him to sit by right in the House of Lords. While Aikman was travelling to Italy the Duke had returned to the Low Countries to fight in the war of the Spanish Succession, distinguishing himself at the battles of Oudenarde and Malplaquet.

Aikman spent time in Florence, where he painted the portrait of the British envoy Sir Henry Newton and his own self-portrait, which soon after was acquired by the

37
WILLIAM AIKMAN

Sir John Clerk of Penicuik, Bt
(1684–1755)

Oil on canvas
50 x 40 (127.0 x 101.6)
Sir John Clerk of Penicuik, Bt

Sir John was the artist's friend and first cousin, their mothers being sisters. He was one of the most distinguished men of his generation, a judge, architect, antiquary and poet. Aikman's letters to his cousin survive and are a most important source of information on the artist. The portrait was probably painted around 1720.

Medici and is now in the Uffizi Gallery. He visited Naples with John Talman, and while in Rome probably studied in one of the leading studios, perhaps Carlo Maratta's, whose work he copied. With introductions from his cousins in Leghorn, Aikman sailed to Turkey, saw Constantinople and painted portraits of the British trading community in Smyrna. He also visited Greece.

A comparison of the works painted by Aikman in Italy with his earlier portraits shows a refining of his style and the emergence of what became the hallmark of his mature portraiture – a certain melancholy and introspection, seen well in the portrait he painted after his return of his cousin and lifelong friend, Baron Clerk [37]. While Medina's men and women are robustly depicted in confidently handled paint and rich colour, Aikman's delicate and tentative portraits penetrate the public mask to the personality behind.

It may have been the news of Medina's death that precipitated Aikman's return to Scotland, for, by March 1711, less than six months after the event, Aikman was back in Edinburgh and had begun to take over Medina's

38
WILLIAM AIKMAN

Allan Ramsay (1686–1758)

Oil on canvas
29$\frac{13}{16}$ x 25$\frac{13}{16}$ (75.7 x 64.0)
Scottish National Portrait Gallery

Ramsay was the leading Scottish poet of the early eighteenth century and a close friend of Aikman and Sir John Clerk. The latter owned this portrait of 1722 and, in imitation of Ramsay's style, wrote the following verse, which he pasted on the back of the canvas:
Here painted on this canvas clout
By Aikman's hand is Ramsay's snout
The picture's value none might doubt
For ten to one I'll venture
The greatest criticks could not tell
Which of the two does most excell
Or in his way should bear the bell
The Poet or the Painter.

39
WILLIAM AIKMAN

Lady Grisel Baillie (1665–1746)

Oil on canvas
30 x 25 (76.2 x 63.5)
The Rt Honble the Earl of Haddington

Lady Grisel Baillie's Household Book records a payment to Aikman in 1717 of £52 for nine original portraits and five copies. This portrait cost Lady Grisel five guineas.

40
WILLIAM AIKMAN

Self-portrait

Oil on canvas
29½ x 24½ (74.9 x 62.2)
Scottish National Portrait Gallery

role as painter to Scotland's aristocracy and gentry [*40*]. He was perfectly placed to do this, for, apart from the elderly John Scougal, there were few others. In addition Aikman belonged to the society that he painted, and his family and friends helped speed the introductions which brought in work. Those friends were men like Duncan Forbes of Culloden, later Lord President of the Court of Session, Sir Gilbert Elliot of Minto and the poet Allan Ramsay [*38*]. Ramsay, a protégé of the Clerks of Penicuik, was an amateur artist, print-dealer, and theatre promoter, as well as the finest Scottish poet of the early eighteenth century. His premises in the Luckenbooths near St Giles were the artistic hub of the capital.

In Edinburgh Aikman charged five guineas for a standard head-and-shoulders portrait – for instance, that of Lady Grisel Baillie [*39*], who sat to him in 1717. Her husband, George, and her daughter, Lady Murray, were painted at the same time. The success of these attractive and accomplished paintings led to further commissions from Lady Grisel's own father, Lord Marchmont, and from her daughter's father-in-law, the Earl of Haddington.

The patronage of the Duke of Argyll was beneficial to Aikman in several ways. It produced business from the

41
WILLIAM AIKMAN

John Hamilton, 4th Lord Belhaven
(died 1764)

Oil on canvas
50 x 40 (127.0 x 101.6)
Charles G. Spence Esq.

Duke himself, who commissioned a great number of portraits for his several houses in England and Scotland. Political associates of Argyll and Campbell kinsmen also commissioned portraits of the Duke, so that there exist today many originals and versions of his portraits.

Aikman was, informally, the Duke's painter, a situation that brought him credit as well as business and helped attract further portrait commissions. Many men, such as John Hamilton, 4th Lord Belhaven, whose portrait Aikman painted in the 1720s [41], were, like the artist, beholden to the Duke of Argyll. Belhaven, for example, owed his position as General of the Mint to the Duke, while his brother inherited his uncle's job of Assistant Solicitor to the Board of Excise. Belhaven complained years later when there was a danger that his brother's salary might be reduced. 'My brother has only half of the salary which his uncle had for that office, & which was erected in a manner for him as a sinecure after the yeare 1715, upon account of his behaviour & my father's that yeare in defence of the present royal family dureing the Rebellion.'[10]

Lord Belhaven, the grandson of the famous peer who opposed the Union, owed his position of General of the Mint to the patronage of the 2nd Duke of Argyll. He later became Sheriff of East Lothian on the recommendation of the 3rd Duke.

57

As early as 1716, soon after the Duke of Argyll had commanded the government forces against the Earl of Mar and the Jacobites, Aikman was contemplating moving south, aware that the immensely successful Sir Godfrey Kneller was seventy and that it could not be long before a younger painter would replace him. With Argyll's backing and his own considerable abilities he had a very good chance to be that man. He decided to move to London in the winter of 1720–21 for an experimental six months. 'I am making what despatch I can with my business here and find my manner pleaseth much . . . I have begunn some fine things to bring in ready money to bear expenses and defray the charge of drapery painters, which are not for ease to be found good in this place as one might have imagin'd. When I am once master of all the Scotch business I brought with me I will know better what to determine as to my continuing here for some tyme longer than I first propos'd.'[11]

Eighteen months later he was settled in London with his wife and children, living in a house off the Haymarket. Immediately his Scottish friends rallied round, using their influence on his behalf. Duncan Forbes, in 1725 appointed Lord Advocate, commissioned a portrait of the Prime Minister, Sir Robert Walpole. 'I have indeed been very busy of late', Aikman wrote to his cousin, Baron Clerk, 'and what I have been about will I hope in a little tyme doe me great service. Amongst other things I have finishd Mr Walpools picture, which is sent home to him and is much approv'n of; there were some people endeavourd to take the advantage of me before the last sitting, and would have discredited it with Mr Walpoll but now its out off their power for he has declared it to be the best picture ever was done for him, next to Sr Godfrey's, and he has satt to all the best masters in towne, this acct I had from Mr Scroup, who you knowe is not ready to exaggerate. To Mr Forbes all this is oweing. The pictur is for him, and he was all the pains to gett Mr Walpool brought to my own house for the last sitting which succeded so well as I have told you. I am extremely oblig'd to Duncan, and if you have occasion to see him pray be so kind as lett him know I told you so.'[12]

As well as the Prime Minister, Aikman had soon painted other leading members of the government, and during the winter of 1723–4 the Earl and Countess of Burlington sat to him. Lord Burlington was England's foremost connoisseur and patron of the arts, and his circle included several of Aikman's friends, in particular William Kent, whom he had met in Italy when Kent had been the travelling companion of John Talman. Back in London, Aikman had painted a full-length portrait of Kent for Lord

JOHN STUART 3ᵈ EARL of BUTE, first Lᵈ of the TREASURY &c &c.

42
WILLIAM AIKMAN
John, 3rd Earl of Bute (1713–92)
Oil on canvas
94 x 57 (238.8 x 144.8)
Private collection

Lord Bute was only ten when his father died, and he spent most of his holidays from Eton at the houses of his Campbell uncles, John, 2nd Duke of Argyll and the Earl of Ilay. The commission for this portrait, a late work of the artist, may have come from the 2nd Duke of Argyll.

Castlemaine's house Wanstead, where Kent had painted a ceiling. Aikman was also commissioned by Lord Burling-ton to paint the portrait of the man he described as 'my great friend', Alexander Pope. Later Pope gave the artist a copy of his translation of the *Odyssey*.

 Another friend of Pope, whom Aikman would almost certainly have known, was the Irish artist Charles Jervas. A few years older than Aikman, he had settled in London by 1709 after a similar period on the Continent. Scottish and Irish art, at the beginning of the eighteenth century, had much in common, and Aikman and Jervas were the two outstanding painters of their respective countries in the first quarter of the century. Both found it necessary to

43
JAMES NORIE
Self-portrait

Oil on canvas
30⅜ x 25 5/16 (77.2 x 64.3)
Royal Scottish Academy

This portrait of Edinburgh's leading landscape and decorative artist has for long been considered to be a self-portrait. If so, it is James Norie's only known portrait.

spend time in London, Jervas returning to Dublin more often than Aikman to Edinburgh. Whereas Jervas was more original in his compositions, Aikman was the more sensitive portrayer of character. Jervas had studied under Kneller, and it was he, in 1723, who succeeded as Principal Painter to the King.

Earlier that year an opportunity had arisen for Aikman when the position of King's Limner for Scotland became vacant on the death of George Ogilvie:

'So soon as I gott notice of Mr Ogilvie's death, as I presumd I knew it amongst the first I wrote to Mr Duncan Forbes, who went immediatly to his Grace of Argyle & Bar. Scroup. The D. of Argyle went to my Lord Town-send and gott his promise, afterwards calld att Mr Walpools but miss'd him, Bar. Scroup found him but too late for he had given him promise to Mr Abercromby of Glassoh, who had an express from Mr Philps of the exchequr, with the news, & made application to Mr Walpool before us. The D. of Argyle was very mad about it & with a very little bad council would have broke his staff, but thank God it is otherwise.'[13]

The Duke's irritation at his failure to obtain a sinecure for

44
THOMAS WARRENDER
Still-life

Oil on canvas
23¼ x 29¼ (59.1 x 74.3)
National Gallery of Scotland

his own artist was natural enough, though threatening to resign his office was an extreme reaction to failure. But Scottish affairs were the Duke's province, and he could not bear interference even in a comparatively minor matter.

While Aikman had a wide clientele and considerable success in London, he was still very much the painter of the Scottish community there. Not only was he the Duke's particular painter but the man chosen by the Duke of Hamilton, the Earl of Stair and many others. Towards the end of his life, when Aikman was beginning to suffer from the tuberculosis that killed him, the young Earl of Bute, the Duke of Argyll's nephew, sat to the painter, who produced a masterpiece of the future Prime Minister wearing Highland dress [42]. Aikman's absence in London during the second half of the 1720s left Edinburgh poorly served for portrait painters. John Scougal had retired in 1715, his uninspired son George continuing in his place. The ablest artist to emerge from Edinburgh during the 1720s was not primarily a portrait painter but a decorative and landscape painter, James Norie [43].

The Nories were a Morayshire family and James was born at Knockando on the Spey, moving south to Edinburgh as a child. He may have been apprenticed to Thomas Warrender [44] and learnt from him his skills in decorative

The painting has a coded political message which is not easy to decipher. The playing cards with two kings of different suits and the arms of England on one and Scotland on the other recall the Union of the two countries in 1707. The pamphlet on the dangers of popery, published in 1708, reinforces the likelihood that the Union is the theme of the painting, since many Presbyterians who subscribed to the National Covenant (shown alongside) saw it as a means of protecting Scotland from Roman Catholicism. The quill pens, both of which point down from these significant documents to the royal images below, may indicate the power of the written word over kings and princes. The seal and its ribbon are those of the burgh of Haddington, Warrender's home town. The document to their left records the date when the artist became a member of his guild.

45
JAMES NORIE

Classical Landscape with
Architecture

Signed and dated: Ja: Norie Edin
1736
Oil on canvas
25½ x 52 (64.8 x 132.0)
National Gallery of Scotland

*This painting is composed from a number
of different engraved sources. The group
of figures is taken from Panini's* View of
the Colosseum, *which pre-dates this
picture by almost twenty years. James
Norie had already copied Panini's figures
in his own capriccio,* View of the Colosseum and Arch of Constantine, *of
1735. The classical ruins on the right
must also have been borrowed from an
engraving, since the image was reversed
and re-used in the following decade when
the Norie firm were working at Keir.*

painting. Unlike William Aikman, James Norie was essentially a tradesman, running a firm that could paint gutters and skirting boards as well as Italianate landscapes [45]. In 1709 James Norie was well enough trained to be admitted freeman of the Incorporated Trades of Edinburgh, and he was soon taking apprentices of his own. From 1718 he was working at Hopetoun, being paid small amounts for painting doors and windows for Charles, the 1st Earl, just as Thomas Warrender had been employed twenty years before by Lord Hopetoun's mother, Lady Margaret Hope. It is indicative of Norie's success that he was able to supplant the older firm, now, after Thomas's retirement in 1710, run by his son John. After 1720 the Warrender business ceased to exist.

James Norie's business dominated decorative painting in Scotland during the first two-thirds of the eighteenth century [fig. 10], but, in retrospect, the firm's success has caused the eclipse of the few other landscape painters who practised. Nearly every piece of generalised, monochromatic landscape found on the walls of eighteenth-century houses has been attributed to Norie, yet there were certainly other artists around. Thomas Kirk painted murals in Inveresk, where, exceptionally, he signed his work; but in general, although the names of many decorative painters are known, their work is anonymous. At Kelburne near Largs and at Woodside House, Beith, there are decorative paintings which stylistically lie outside the Norie tradition. Perhaps these and other Ayrshire houses were decorated from Glasgow, a city which was growing fast in the eighteenth century but about whose painters too little is known. No decorative paintings by even such a well-established firm as the Warrenders have

ever been identified, yet it is recorded that they painted them. It is likely that they still exist, but attributed to Norie.

While misattributions have caused confusion, the difficulties of studying eighteenth-century Scottish decorative painting are compounded by the problem of differentiating the styles of the various members of the Norie family themselves. As well as James Norie, the founder of the firm, there were three sons, at least two of whom were artists, James Norie junior, born in 1711, and his younger brother, Robert.

James junior, with his father, signed the Charter of the Edinburgh Academy of St Luke in 1729. He was then eighteen and presumably attended the drawing classes there. Later he studied in London under the scene and landscape painter George Lambert, and was considered at his very early death in 1736 to have been an exceptionally talented painter. Yet there are no works that can be securely attributed to him. A group of landscapes, the finest produced by the Nories, are signed James Norie and dated between 1731 and 1736, but they could as well be by the father as by the son [45–47]. Robert was a much less able painter. Several works are signed and dated by him, in particular a newly discovered pair of landscapes found in a house in Dumfries of 1744. They have none of the sophistication of the earlier landscapes; the figures are poorly proportioned and the perspective faulty. No wonder that the Dutchman Isaak Vogelsang left a successful practice in Ireland to try his luck in Scotland. He was disappointed, however, for the Scots, unlike the Irish, had little interest in landscape painting. While talented painters, native and foreign, depicted the towns and

46
JAMES NORIE
Classical Landscape with Trees and Lake
Signed and dated: Ja:Norie Edin 1736
Oil on canvas
25½ x 52 (64.8 x 132.0)
National Gallery of Scotland

A pair to [45]. Although both paintings are signed it is impossible to know whether they were painted by the father or the son. The figures are likely to have been copied from prints.

Fig. 10
James Norie's trade card. On loan to Aberdeen University Library, Montcoffer Papers A/145. Reproduced by permission of Captain Ramsay of Mar

47
JAMES NORIE

A Landscape with Women Bathing

Signed and dated: James Norie
Edin 1736
Oil on canvas
26 x 53¼ (66.0 x 135.3)
Aberdeen Art Gallery and
Museums

48

DAVID MURRAY (ACTIVE 1733)

The Honourable Company of
Hunters

Oil on canvas
26 x 31½ (66.0 x 80.0)
National Trust for Scotland, The
House of The Binns

*The Hunt appears to be the forerunner of
the Royal Caledonian Hunt, which was
founded as the Hunt Club in 1777 and
changed its name to the Caledonian
Hunt a year later.*

countryside of Ireland, little comparable work was produced in Scotland [48]. Indeed, during the eighteenth century, while Scottish portraiture was at least the equal if not superior to Irish portraiture, landscape painting was markedly inferior and for the whole of the century Scotland trailed Ireland by at least a generation.

There are very few topographical paintings which date from the first half of the eighteenth century. One of the most interesting is the great view of Wemyss Castle and the Fife coast which, judging from the flags on the ships, was painted before the Union. The artist was almost certainly foreign, probably Dutch. In the early 1740s, when Lord Belhaven was enlarging Biel, his house near Dunbar, he commissioned the Nories to paint the view

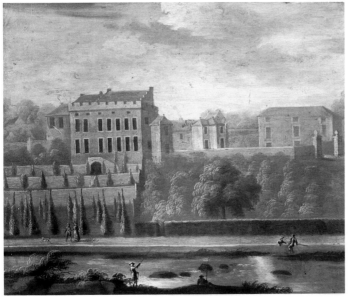

49
JAMES NORIE

Panorama of Taymouth Castle and
Loch Tay

Oil on canvas
26 x 52⅜ (66.0 x 133.0)
Scottish National Portrait Gallery

*James Norie was paid £9 in September
1733 by John Campbell, Lord Glenorchy,
for painting this view of his property. In
1739 the picture was partly repainted by
Jan Griffier II to show the changes that
had been made to the landscaped park in
the intervening six years. Griffier's dark
green repaint is clearly visible.*

50
JAMES NORIE

Biel House

Oil on panel
37 x 45 (94.0 x 114.0)
Charles G. Spence Esq.

from the Biel burn [50]. Typical of much of their work, it
is in grisaille, suggesting that it formed the centrepiece of a
larger scheme of decoration.

James Norie's panorama of Taymouth Castle and Loch
Tay [49] was painted for John Campbell, Lord Glenorchy,
in 1733. More sophisticated than the view of Biel, it was
nevertheless considered by Glenorchy to be a work of
topography rather than fine art, for within six years he had
commissioned another artist to repaint it to show the
changes he had made to his park and gardens.

The designer of the Taymouth gardens as well as the
architect of its new pavilions was William Adam, and until
his death in 1748 there was a close business connection

*This view of Biel near Dunbar was pain-
ted in grisaille, probably in the 1740s, as
part of a decorative scheme for the owner,
John, 4th Lord Belhaven [41]. It is
impossible to be certain which member of
the Norie firm painted it. The painting
shows the probably sixteenth-century
tower house, enlarged in the late seventeenth century, when the terraced garden
was also created. The large building on
the right is probably by William Adam,
who in the 1740s was designing another
house for Lord Belhaven.*

Fig. 11

Decorative landscape at Caroline Park, Edinburgh, by James Norie. Over the frame is the monogram A for Argyll surmounted by a ducal coronet. To the sides are a pair of lions, the supporters of the Argyll coat of arms. Reproduced by permission of the Royal Commission on the Ancient and Historical Monuments of Scotland

between Adam's building and architectural firm and the Nories. Where Adam built, Norie generally decorated, and the list of the houses where both were at work – Arniston, Haddo, Hopetoun, Mavisbank and Yester, for instance – reads like a catalogue of the greatest architectural projects of the period. One scheme where both men were involved was at Royston House in the parish of Cramond, which the 2nd Duke of Argyll bought for his daughter in 1739 and renamed Caroline Park. There the Norie family were given their most extensive commission, working in several rooms, on plaster and on panel, their grandest landscapes surrounded by painted swags, trophies, coronets and coats of arms [fig. 11].

The Duke [fig. 12] had been a good friend to Scottish artists, and although much of his life had been lived out of Scotland, he was at pains to promote and protect his fellow countrymen. The architect James Gibbs, as a Roman Catholic and Jacobite, might have expected little from the Protestant, Hanoverian Duke, but Gibbs designed the Duke's magnificent Sudbroke House and worked for him

Fig. 12
The monument to John, 2nd Duke of Argyll, in Westminster Abbey, by L. F. Roubiliac. Copyright A. F. Kersting

at Adderbury in Oxfordshire. Gibbs dedicated his publication, *A Book of Architecture*, to the Duke because, as Aikman and others might have put it, of the 'early encouragement I received from your Grace, in my profession upon my return from *Italy* and the honour of your protection ever since.'

Clan Grant

Richard Waitt, John Smibert and the patronage of Clan Grant

At the end of the year 1710 Ludovic Grant of Grant, in his late sixties, reviewed his great Highland clan, drawn up before him in their traditional place of rendezvous and justice at Balintome in Strathspey. His son Alexander had issued an order that 'all the gentlemen and commons of his name wear whiskers, and make all their plaids and tartan of red and green.' He 'commanded them all to appear before him . . . in that uniform, in kilt and under arms, which order was complied with.'[14]

The Chieftain for forty-seven years was handing over leadership of his clan to his eldest son. He made a speech resigning his authority, commending his son to the clan and exhorting them, in return, to maintain 'the same good character, with regard to courage and unanimity, which they bore while he commanded them.'

There had been Grants in the Highlands from at least the thirteenth century, and since the fifteenth their centre had been at Freuchie in Strathspey. Ludovic Grant was 8th Laird of Freuchie but, in recognition of the increasing importance of the clan and as a reward for their unyielding Presbyterian faith and support, King William issued a charter in 1694 stating that Ludovic and his heirs would from henceforth style themselves Lairds of Grant, that Freuchie would become the Burgh of Grant (or Grantown), the House of Freuchie be named Castle Grant, and that the clan lands would become the Regality of Grant.

After five hundred years in the Highlands there were many families who called themselves Grant. They could be kinsmen or tenants and in many cases both. It was the men of these families who appeared in military order at Balintome, perhaps as many as three hundred, men like George Grant of Cleurie, Mungo Grant of Mullochard, Patrick Grant of Tullochgriban. With them would have been the laird's piper, William Cummine [51], not a Grant himself, but a member of a celebrated family of hereditary

51
RICHARD WAITT

William Cummine, the Piper of the
Laird of Grant (dates not known)

Signed and dated: Ric. Waitt. ad
vivum Pinxit 1714
Oil on canvas
84 x 60½ (213.4 x 153.7)
National Museums of Scotland

*Waitt was paid £5 in January 1715 for
this portrait commissioned by Alexander
Grant, Chief of Clan Grant. In contrast
to modern practice, Cummine supports
his pipes on his right shoulder. The pipe
banner shows the chief's coat of arms and
motto, 'Standfast'. In the background
Waitt has shown Castle Grant, not as it
was at the time but with the right wing of
the main block made symmetrical, a project of the laird which was never carried
out. Like the Champion, the Piper is
dressed in livery. This would have been
supplied by the laird in the same way that
Macleod of Macleod ordered a set of livery
for his principal piper, MacCrimmon, in
1714; it was supplied by Patrick Mor-
rison of Edinburgh.*

musicians. Also present must have been Alastair Grant
Mor, the Laird's Champion [52], and all the other men
and boys who made up the Chief's retinue of his standard-
bearer, gentlemen of the name, bard, armour bearer and
his many gillies.

Like many of their fellow Highland chiefs the Grants still
maintained a traditional Celtic court where the arts of
poetry and music flourished. Until the middle of the
seventeenth century such families had sent their bards and
harpists to Ireland, which shared a common Gaelic
culture. But the flow back and forth from the Highlands to
Ireland was finally broken in mid-century when Cromwell
destroyed Ireland's Gaelic civilisation forcing Scottish
poets and musicians to train at home. The bagpipe was
beginning to replace the harp from the turn of the
seventeenth century as the favoured instrument in the
courts of the Highland chieftains. Pipers like the Cum-
mines were sent to acquire their skills from the leading

52
RICHARD WAITT

Alastair Grant Mor, the Champion
of the Laird of Grant
(dates not known)

Signed and dated: Ric Waitt ad
vivum pinxit 1714
Oil on canvas
86 x 63½ (218.4 x 161.3)
The Honble Viscount Reidhaven

piping families of Scotland such as the MacGregors of
Glenlyon, well known in their day as the *Clann an
Sgeulaiche*, or the MacCrimmons of Skye. What makes the
Grants so exceptional was not that they still maintained a
traditional Highland court with poets, musicians and
warrior champions, but that they employed an artist,
Richard Waitt, to record it.

Waitt was first employed by the clan three years after the
review at Balintome, when he painted the new laird,
Alexander, and his brother, Colonel Lewis Grant. In 1713
or 1714 Alexander commissioned the artist to paint his
sister, Margaret, and another brother, George; but the
most impressive pictures he ordered were the companion
full-lengths of his Piper and Champion which Waitt
painted for the laird in 1714. These magnificent portraits
cost £5 a piece, in contrast to the portraits of Alexander,
his brothers and sister, which were much more modest
and cost a mere guinea each. All these portraits were

*A senior member of the Chief's retinue,
the Champion wears livery, his tartan
similar to that of the piper. He is well
armed with a long-barrelled musket,
pistol, dirk and scimitar-bladed sword.
The latter is of a type not unknown in the
Highlands at this time; Stewart of Ard-
shiel had a similar one which was described as a 'claymore called the Turk'.
Local tradition preserves the memory
that this heroic and seemingly archaic
figure was in fact a pioneer of modern
building techniques, being the first person
in Strathspey to have a lime-mortared
and slated dwelling house built for
himself.*

71

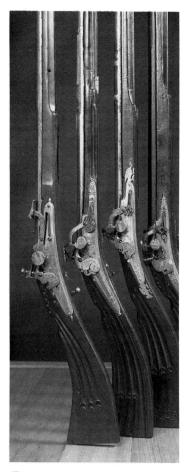

Fig. 13
Guns from the armoury of Castle Grant.
Reproduced by permission of the Trustees
of the National Museums of Scotland

acquired by the laird to form the nucleus of a clan portrait gallery at Castle Grant. Meanwhile Richard Waitt was also painting portraits of the laird's kinsmen and tenants in chief, the heads of those families who had offered their loyalty to their new chief at Balintome.

In 1713 Waitt painted portraits of the brothers Alexander Grant of Grantsfield and Ludovic Grant of Knockando, second cousins of the laird. He painted James Grant of Wester Elchies, his first cousin, Patrick Grant of Miltown, his hereditary standard-bearer, as well as Grant of Cleurie, Delay, Delboyak, Mullochard and Tullochgriban. More members of the clan were painted the following year.

No other family in Scotland, or in Europe for that matter, commissioned a similar group of portraits of their clan – family, retainers and kinsmen – and it is as a group rather than as individual paintings that Waitt's portraits of Clan Grant should be judged. Sadly Castle Grant, its great armoury [fig. 13] and these portraits have been separated, but together their combined effect was impressive.

'Everything without and within denotes the habitation of a Chieftain, and brings to remembrance those days, in which the head of every tribe was surrounded by his own clan. His castle was their fortress; his approbation was their pride; his protection was both their duty and their interest. In his safety their own fate was involved.'[15]

Little enough is known about the artist Richard Waitt. With such constant support from Clan Grant throughout his career, it might be supposed that he was a Highlander – his surname is not unknown in the North-East. But there is nothing to prove or disprove this. The first notice of him is in April 1707, when he was married in Edinburgh to Margaret, the daughter of a prominent non-juring Episcopal minister, David Freebairn, who became a bishop and died Primus of the Episcopal Church in 1739. The Freebairns, like many Episcopalian families, were Jacobites. Margaret's brother James fought in the 1715 Rising, and it is quite possible that Richard Waitt shared his convictions. If so, he would have been on the opposite side politically to the Presbyterian Grants, determined as they were on the Protestant succession and firm supporters of the claim of the house of Hanover against the Stewarts.

Waitt's first recorded work dates from 1708, the year following his marriage, when he was paid for painting the arms of the Earl of Hopetoun in the church at Abercorn. Portraits signed and dated by him of 1710 (Bethia Dundas) and 1713 (Patrick Smythe) support the tradition that Waitt was trained by the Edinburgh painter John Scougal. Not only are they similar in style to Scougal's work but they show members of families that John Scougal had already painted.

Fig. 14
Baltus Barents van Kleek, by Richard Waitt. Fred J. Johnston

Whereas Waitt's activities and sitters up to about 1712 suggest that he may have worked from a studio in Edinburgh, it is hard to believe that the Grant portraits were painted there. Perhaps the Laird of Grant offered him accommodation or he had premises in Elgin or Inverness where his sitters could call [53]. But what happened to Waitt in the years following 1715, when the Grant commission came to an end, is even more of a mystery. Apart from a single portrait dated 1716, there is nothing between then and 1722 to suggest where he was or what he was doing. The one surviving painting is itself a puzzle, for it is supposed to represent the Dutchman Baltus Barents van Kleek, who settled in the American colonies, built a house for himself at Poughkeepsie and died in 1717 [fig. 14]. If the portrait does show van Kleek, and there are considerable doubts about this, then Waitt himself may have emigrated after the Jacobite Rising.

If this is the case he was not the only Scottish artist in the American colonies at that time. John Watson had arrived a year or so before and had settled at Perth Amboy, where he drew and painted some of the Scottish community and others in New Jersey, a state particularly favoured by

73

53
RICHARD WAITT

Sir Archibald Grant of Monymusk,
Bt (1697–1778)

Signed and dated: Ric Waitt pinxit
1715
Oil on canvas
29¼ x 25 (74.0 x 63.5)
The Queen's Body Guard for
Scotland (Royal Company of
Archers)

*Until recently described as a portrait of
Archibald Burnett of Carlops, the painting was correctly identified by the author
of an article on Newhall House in vol VII
of the Scottish Antiquary (1893): 'The
subject is understood to be – Grant,
younger of Cullen. It bears on the canvas
Ric Waitt, pinxit 1715.' Archibald was
the eldest son of Sir Francis Grant, Lord
Cullen, and the portrait shows him in
Archer's uniform. The portrait com-
memorates two recent events in the sitter's life. On 4 October 1714 he was
admitted an Archer, and the following
month he was called to the Bar. Parliament Hall in Parliament Square, where
Grant would have practised as an advocate, is the setting of this portrait.*

French Huguenots and Scots. Later, in 1725, an artist
called Chambers, who had worked for Sir John de Medina
in Edinburgh and then as William Aikman's assistant in
London, arrived in New York, where he stayed for ten
years before returning to Britain. But apart from one
doubtfully identified portrait, there is no trace of Richard
Waitt in the colonies, no examples of his distinctive
portraits, which are superior in characterisation and technique to any painted in North America at that date.

In 1729 another Scottish artist arrived in the colonies
with the intention of settling permanently. John Smibert
had been working in London, but in the words of a
contemporary 'he could not well relish the false selfish
griping overreaching ways too commonly practiz'd
here.'[16] This somewhat idealistic Scot decided to join
George Berkeley, Dean of Derry, and his party, who were
leaving Britain to found a college in Bermuda, the aim of
which was the conversion and education of the American
Indians. They landed in Virginia and sailed north to
Rhode Island, where the Dean intended to buy farm land
to support his college. After about six months Smibert
moved to Boston, where he settled, married and became
one of the most successful artists in the colonies.

He had been born in Edinburgh, his father's family coming from Middleton, just south of Gorebridge. He was trained by the little-known house painter Walter Marshall. In 1709, on the completion of his apprenticeship, Smibert travelled to London and studied at the same academy that Aikman had attended a few years earlier. He had a job as a coach painter. Smibert was back in Edinburgh in 1716, and the following year he was painting members of the Grant family. These were the Grants of Monymusk, a cadet branch of the Grants of Grant, Sir Francis Grant, Smibert's patron, being the son of Archibald Grant of Ballintomb near Knockando. Sir Francis was one of the ablest lawyers of his generation and had earned quick promotion and a baronetcy. He took his seat on the bench in 1709 as Lord Cullen. Four years later he bought from Sir William Forbes of Pitsligo the House of Monymusk, which has remained in the family ever since.

Smibert painted several portraits of members of the family of Lord Cullen. All seem to be in one way or another auxiliary to the great family group [54], which shows the judge surrounded by his children. Archibald, his eldest son, is on the right with his wife, Anne Hamilton, whom he married in 1717, and their baby, the judge's grandchild. Standing beside Alexander are his two brothers: nearest is William, later the judge Lord Prestongrange, and then Francis, who became a merchant. Seated on the other side of the room is Lord Cullen's eldest

54
JOHN SMIBERT

Sir Francis Grant, Lord Cullen, and His Family

Oil on canvas
83 x 129½ (210.8 x 328.9)
Sir Archibald Grant of Monymusk, Bt

Smibert painted a number of portraits of Lord Cullen's family which appear to be connected with this very large group portrait. It is difficult to date. Lord Cullen's full achievement is shown prominently over the door in the centre of the painting, his coat of arms held up by supporters which he was not granted until 1720. By then Smibert was in Italy, not returning to London until 1722, when he would have had little time to pay a visit to Edinburgh. Yet the style of the portrait and the ages of the sitters (Archibald, on the right-hand side, married Anne Hamilton in 1717, and their infant son is shown beside them) suggest that the picture was painted before Smibert left Edinburgh in 1719. The possibility remains that the portrait was painted in 1718 or 1719 and that the angel supporters were added later.

75

55
JOHN SMIBERT

Modello for Lord Cullen's family
portrait

Oil on canvas
17 x 27¾ (43.2 x 70.5)
Sir Archibald Grant of Monymusk,
Bt

*The sitters appear to be a year or two
younger than in the larger portrait* [54].

daughter, Jean, with her husband, Alexander Garden of
Troup, and behind them Jean's four younger sisters,
Christian, Helen, Anne and Sarah. As Lord Cullen's first
two wives were dead, they are represented by their framed
portraits. Jean Grant's portrait is the one by John Scougal
painted in 1700 [35].

Smibert made a preliminary oil sketch or modello for this
large and ambitious canvas [55], but although the finished
painting follows the modello in the grouping of the
figures, it has been reduced, so that it no longer shows the
legs of most of the family or the floor. It might be
supposed that the larger picture had been cut down, but
the same difference between modello and finished painting occurs in Smibert's later Bermuda group, which shows
George Berkeley, the artist and other associates of the
Dean's American project. Perhaps Smibert felt it easier to
compose such complex groups showing the bodies complete in their perspectival space and then, when he had
successfully achieved a natural grouping, he would com-
press the composition, confident that his figures would be
correctly and naturally positioned.

It is possible that the modello for the family group was
painted in Edinburgh during 1718 or the first half of 1719.
The large picture was probably not completed until after
Smibert's return from Italy in August 1722. In 1720 Lord
Cullen was granted supporters to his coat of arms, and
these are clearly shown on the larger painting. They also
appear on the modello, but may have been painted in later.

56
JOHN SMIBERT
Allan Ramsay (1686–1758)
Oil on canvas
24 x 20¼ (61.0 x 51.3)
Private collection

While Smibert was in Scotland one of his greatest friends was Allan Ramsay. Between 1716 and 1719 Smibert painted two portraits of the poet, one full-face, which he took with him to Italy to be engraved, and which is now lost, and a second, profile portrait, which has recently been rediscovered [56]. This second portrait of Ramsay, hitherto known from a crude copy, is very fluently painted, proving that when Smibert left Edinburgh for Italy on 1 August 1719 he was not, like Aikman twelve years earlier, going there as a student but, at the age of thirty-one, as an accomplished artist in his own right. Naturally he would benefit from copying the old masters in the ducal gallery in Florence or from seeing the churches and studios of Rome, but another reason for his Italian journey, perhaps the primary reason, was to buy works of art.

During his first year in Florence, Smibert spent almost £450 on paintings by Romanelli, Dandini, Marinari and Volterrano, as well as flower-pieces, drawings and pietra dura boxes. He spent more money on these works of art than he ever made in a single year as an artist. Given his modest background it is unlikely he had much money of his own to spend. Such purchases suggest financial backing from someone like Lord Cullen who wanted to buy fashionable paintings and objets d'art to furnish his house.

Allan Ramsay, the poet and father of the painter, was a contemporary and friend of Smibert, who painted him at least twice. One portrait is known only from the engraving after it, published as the frontispiece of Ramsay's Poems *of 1721. That and this portrait were probably painted in Edinburgh between 1716 and 1719. Smibert had one of his portraits of Ramsay with him in Boston, possibly exhibited in his showroom in Queen Street (now called Court Street). A portrait of Ramsay by Smibert was owned by A. B. Grosart in 1847, but it is impossible to say if the Boston and the Grosart portraits are the same, or if either is this work.*

57
JOHN SMIBERT

Sir Archibald and Lady Grant of
Monymusk

Oil on canvas
56 x 66 (142.2 x 167.7)
Sir Archibald Grant of Monymusk,
Bt

Smibert's notebook reveals that this most
elegant double portrait, 'Sir Archibald
Grant and Lady in one cloth', was pain-
ted in May 1727. Smibert asked thirty-
two guineas, the price he also charged for
a full-length, but he appears to have had
difficulties in getting Sir Archibald to
pay.

Another possibility is that Smibert was buying for resale in
Britain. While he was in Rome he met Andrew Hay, a man
he would have known as a Medina pupil in Edinburgh.
Hay was one of the first art dealers in Britain, and he
bought on the Continent to sell at auction in London. Hay
and Smibert may have had a business agreement.

While in Italy, Allan Ramsay had written his friend a
poem, the last lines of which suggest that he believed that
Smibert would be returning to Scotland. It is likely that he
did, if just to finish the Grant family portrait, but in August
1722 Smibert was established in London 'on a level with
some of the best painters.'[17] He had a flourishing portrait
practice, and in 1727, the year after Lord Cullen's death,
Archibald the new baronet and his wife sat to him in his
Covent Garden studio. The result was an excellent double
portrait of the young couple, original in composition,
elegant and informal [57].

Sir Archibald and Lady Grant were living at this time in
Greenwich, in a house they rented from the widow of the
architect and playwright Sir John Vanbrugh. In the year
the double portrait was painted, Sir Archibald, the Member

of Parliament for Aberdeenshire, became heavily indebted to his stockbroker and started to speculate in the funds of a charity of which he was a director. By 1731 he and his partners had lost the whole of its capital, leaving it with liabilities of over £450,000. Smibert had emigrated in 1728, and a letter he wrote to Sir Archibald from Boston on 19 January 1734 suggests that the bill for the double portrait had still not been paid.

'Dear Sir

'I received yours of September the 11th & am heartily sory for your misfortunes & can assure you, I should be glad of any oportunity wherein I could be of use to you & if your interest & inclinations should occasion your coming over here; you wil find me readier in deeds than words. The narrowness of my fortune wil not allow me to be so generous as my inclinations are, my family has increased & is likely to hold on, besides I have met with some considerable pulbacks, that has brought me a little behind hand, so that I can not without hurting my family make so large an abatement, as I should otherwise chear-

58
WILLIAM ROBERTSON

The Family of Sir Archibald Grant of Monymusk

Oil on canvas
26 x 30¼ (66.0 x 76.8)
Sir Archibald Grant of Monymusk, Bt

Painted in the early 1740s, the portrait shows the children of the 2nd Baronet and his second wife, Anne Potts. Their eldest son, Archibald (1731–96), is seated at the table drawing fortifications; his brother William (died 1755) stands beside him. In the background is a remarkable cabinet of scientific instruments collected by Sir Archibald, whose widespread interests included mathematics, science and agricultural improvements.

59

RICHARD WAITT

Nic Ciarain, the Henwife of Castle Grant (dates not known)

Signed and dated: Ric Waitt pinxit 17 6

Oil on canvas

30 x 25 (76.2 x 63.5)

The Rt Honble the Earl of Seafield

The last item on Waitt's bill of 26 October 1726 reads: 'For old Naikairn her picture'. The price was 25 shillings. 'Naikairn' is a rendering of a Gaelic surname which Waitt had heard and written down phonetically. The Henwife was probably the daughter of the son of (Nic) Ciaran, or possibly Eachairn. Alternatively the name may incorporate a place-name (for example, Nighean a Chairn), denoting that her family tenanted a farm called The Cairn. She wears a kertch, a headdress popular in the seventeenth and early eighteenth centuries. Her shawl, or tonnag, is fastened with a circular Highland brooch, probably of brass. The date inscribed on the portrait is incorrect.

fuly do; however knowing your friendship to me, I leave it with you to make the abatement as litle as maybe, but if your circumstances requires it, I wil forgive ye interest & be satisfied with the principal, which is about as much as you desired. Mr Hucks has the bond & the management of all my money, so I desire you would pay it to him by mid summer acording to your proposal; my affairs are ordered so that a disapointment would be of damage to me. In a former letter I wrote you my design of buying a farm about 10 or 12 miles from this town, but my friends diswaded me from it, a country life being what I never had tried and I am entirely a stranger to farming, so I gave over the project, at least for the present. I have now got into a house of my Father in laws, who has built me a large and handsome painting room & show room in al[l] respects to my satisfaction. My family is weell & sallute you & yours [58]. I hope to see, or at least hear of your being in more flourishing circumstances. I am Dear Sir Your most sincere friend & serv^t: John Smibert.'[18]

Sir Archibald's kinsman Sir James Grant of Grant, brother of Alexander and son of Ludovic Grant of Grant, was the Member of Parliament for Inverness-shire. The only

60
RICHARD WAITT
General James Grant of
Ballindalloch as a child (1720–1806)
Signed and dated: Ric Waitt Pinxt
1726
Oil on canvas
51½ x 25 ⅖ (131.0 x 64.5)
Mrs Oliver Russell

speech he is recorded as having made in the House was in
May 1732, asking for clemency for his kinsman. Following
the deaths of both his father and brother, Sir James, who
had acquired his baronetcy with his Colquhoun bride, was
now Laird of Grant himself, and he soon resumed his
family's patronage of Richard Waitt.

A bill of 1726 lists the portraits which Sir James had
commissioned. The most expensive was a double portrait
of the new laird and his wife, though at £6 this was far
cheaper than Smibert's price of thirty-two guineas for Sir
Archibald and Lady Grant's picture. Waitt was a very
inexpensive artist. He still charged only a guinea for a
standard head-and-shoulders portrait at a time when
William Aikman, by no means the most expensive painter
in London, was about to raise his price for a full-length
from thirty to forty guineas. As well as the double portrait
of Sir James and his wife, Waitt painted several of their
children. The list of portraits on Waitt's bill ends with the
line 'For old Naikairn her picture £01-05-00', presumably
the entry for the portrait of the Henwife of Castle Grant

*This portrait of the Laird of Grant's
nephew James was painted when he was
five. The fort in the background may be
meant to represent Edinburgh Castle.*

81

61

RICHARD WAITT

A Still-life of Cauliflowers, Poultry
and a Leg of Mutton

Signed and dated: R. Waitt pinxit
1724

Oil on canvas

23¼ x 30⅞ (59.3 x 78.5)

National Gallery of Scotland

*Although this is the only still-life by
Waitt known today, it is unlikely that so
accomplished a painting was unique in
his work. The 1733 inventory of the
Marquess of Annandale's collection, compiled by Andrew Hay and John Alexander, lists 'A still life by Mr Richard
Watt £2-2-0.' But it is impossible to
know whether that refers to this painting
or another.*

[59]. Smaller than the portraits of the Piper and the
Champion [51, 52], it is yet another extraordinary image
of one of the clan retainers. As an unidealised portrait of
one of the people, it is unique in Scottish art of its date;
only Medina's and Aikman's portraits of the butlers at
Wemyss Castle of 1702 and 1722 respectively are in any
way comparable, and they represent the upper servant of
the household rather than the lower world out of doors.
Waitt's Henwife too has none of the condescending
humour which characterises continental portraits of the
peasantry.

Just as, ten years earlier, Alexander Grant had encouraged
his kinsmen to send their portraits to him, so, under the
new laird, more portraits of Grants were hung at the
castle. In two cases, portraits of the sons of men who had
been painted earlier were sent: George Grant, son of
Patrick Grant of Tullochgorm, and Robert, son of Donald
Grant of Glenbeg. Portraits of the Grant of Tulloch, of
Riemore, Burnside and Carron followed. Patrick Grant of
Easter Elchies, later the judge Lord Elchies, sent his.
Several of the Laird's richer relations, the Grants of
Rothiemurcus and the Roses of Kilravock, for instance,
commissioned their own group of family portraits from

62
RICHARD WAITT
Self-portrait
Signed and dated on the easel: Ric
Waitt Pictor ipse pinxit 1728
Oil on canvas
42 x 50 (60.7 x 127.0)
Scottish National Portrait Gallery

Until bought by the Scottish National Portrait Gallery in 1968, this painting was owned by the family of Rose of Kilravock, good patrons of Waitt in the latter years of his life. Faulty in perspective, it is nevertheless a compelling image, the most ambitious Scottish self-portrait since George Jamesone painted his in the late 1630s. [Reproduced in colour on the back cover.]

Waitt. So did Sir James's sister Anne, married to Colonel William Grant of Ballindalloch, a couple to whom the Laird entrusted much of the responsibility for running his estates while he was away from the Highlands.

In 1726 Waitt painted three of their children, including the appealing portrait of the future soldier, conqueror of St Lucia and governor of Florida, James Grant [60]. Besides its considerable charm, it shows Waitt's ability to use every square inch of his canvas, so that the spaces round the figure have a tension which gives liveliness to the whole design. This confidence to think of his pictures two-dimensionally, like court cards, is new in Waitt's work and begs the questions where he was and what he was doing between 1716 and 1721.

Two paintings of the 1720s suggest that Waitt was a more varied painter than he now appears. One of these is his accomplished still-life of vegetables, meat and bread laid on a plain larder shelf [61]. It would be surprising if so skilful a painting was unique in his work. The other intriguing picture is his own self-portrait of 1728, where the artist is shown at his easel, pointing to a picture he has just completed [62]. Waitt's prototype for this unusual picture was a painting that was almost certainly at Castle Grant in his day. This is George Jamesone's self-portrait, where the early seventeenth-century artist is also shown, palette in hand, pointing to his own work. But is the canvas on Waitt's easel an example of a type of work the artist painted but which no longer survives? It is more likely that the rather lumpen female, who gazes at the painter rather than the mirror in her hand, symbolises the art of portraiture itself.

Duff and Gordon

John Alexander, William Mosman and the patronage of the Duffs and Gordons

John Alexander and William Mosman were both natives of Aberdeen, and throughout their long and similar careers it was the patronage of that city and of the families of the North-East which helped train, maintain and provide them with their greatest commissions. The Duffs were Mosman's most important patrons, while the Earl of Mar and the Dukes of Gordon were Alexander's.

John Alexander was born in 1686, the son of an Aberdeen doctor. His great-grandfather was George Jamesone, the most famous Scottish painter of the early seventeenth century. Nothing is known of Alexander's early life until 1710, when he is recorded working in London. The following year he painted a self-portrait miniature. He was then at Leghorn, having, as he wrote on the back of the miniature, just arrived there by sea from London, aged twenty-five, *en route* to study in Florence and Rome. It is likely that he trained in London as a miniature painter, and possibly in Paris as well. George Vertue, who knew him personally, described him a few years later as 'a merry dispos'd gent, laughs eternally.' The Marquess of Annandale, who may have known him better, described him in a moment of exasperation as 'a foolish simple body'. The Marquess was engaged in creating a magnificent collection of Italian paintings and sculpture, and Alexander, in Rome, helped him. He also made drawings of works of art for Annandale, but George Ross, rather than Alexander, seems to have been his painter in Italy, copying the Guido Renis in the Colonna and Barberini collections.

Alexander probably travelled to Italy at his own expense. He lived on the money he earned working for British visitors to Rome, supplemented by what his father could afford to send him. He remained there for ten years, studying alongside William Kent with one of the leading Roman painters of the day, Giuseppe Bartolomeo Chiari.

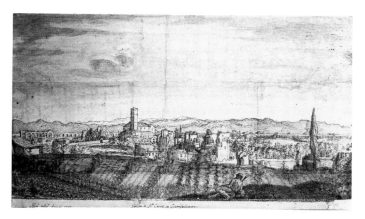

He drew from the life at the French Academy and copied the works of Raphael. His few surviving Roman drawings, figure and landscape [fig. 15], and his set of engravings after Raphael's frescoes in the Vatican show considerable ability, and he appears to have been well thought of by Chiari, who gave him one of his drawings.

Two political events transformed the second half of Alexander's time in Rome. The first was the failure of the Jacobite Rising of 1715 and the consequent exile of its leader, the Earl of Mar; the second was the removal of the Jacobite court, first to Urbino and finally to Rome. As a Roman Catholic and Jacobite, Alexander benefited from both of these events. Lord Mar was with the court in Urbino when Alexander wrote to him in June 1718: 'I received your letter, while I was busy about the drawings of the two little ovals, which I shall send in a letter next post ... I hope the stories will please you, if my weak performance and ideas answer your bon gusto ... One represents Perseus cutting off Medusa's head and the other Perseus delivering Andromeda. I had a genio [inspiration] to do these two stories, because I found them applicable to your Grace in the last conjuncture you had in Scotland.'

Alexander was already painting, probably commissioned by Lord Mar, for the exiled royal family. 'You will receive from the post the Parnassus of Raphael ... I pray you anew to excuse my weak beginnings to the King. I suppose critics will see my picture and, that they may not criticise what is not faulty, I confess it is three years since I painted it, and at that time I lived on my own industry and the small money my father could send me, so I could not go to the expense of fine ultra marine, which is the cause the blues are not so beautiful. For the rest I have copied the original even to the least herbs and that to an error, if Raphael was capable of making any.'[19]

Ten days later, after discussing some commissions he had undertaken for Lord Mar, Alexander continued: 'I find I have not the patience I was wont to have in little; notwithstanding, when you command me, I shall undertake anything, though never so difficult, because I surpass myself, when I labour for those I esteem and love, for which reason I hope to succeed in the life of Mary Stuart, that great Queen, for if my performance could equal my love and esteem for her glorious memory, I am confident I should equal Raphael and Titian. I am ambitious to be able one day to represent her glorious actions and sufferings, as Rubens has done that of Mary de Medici.'[20]

Alexander was not alone in finding a parallel between the fate of Mary in the sixteenth century and the contemporary plight of the Jacobite royal family. In July 1718 he wrote again to Mar: 'I should be very glad to receive the favour you promised me of Mr Crafurd's book, for I never read anything concerning that great Queen but Floremond Remond in his book La Naissance et Cadence de L'Heresie and a compend in Italian taken, I suppose from Caussin's Holy Court.' After presenting the compliments of Trevisani, who had recently painted the Earl's portrait, Alexander continued: 'I heartily wish the King to take a lady and make her become the mistress and queen of nations, that there may be a fit companion to be painted on the same cloth with his Majesty and that she not only be a fine model for the painter, but, what is most important, she prove a good mould, that the King and she may give us many brave young masters. I pray that, when his Majesty shall give us a queen, God will bless them with all the blessings that the Roman Catholic Church pronounces on these occasions.'[21]

The following year, in answer to the wishes of many other Jacobites, James Francis Edward Stewart, the Old Pretender, married the Polish heiress and princess Clementina Sobieska. She was the god-daughter of Pope Clement XI, and he gave the young royal couple the Palazzo Muti in the Piazza Ss. Apostoli, which then became the centre of the Jacobite court in Rome. The Pope also commissioned Chiari to paint an altarpiece for the Stewarts. This still exists in Rome. Its subject is an allegory of the Church, and it shows Faith, Hope and Charity in a small boat steered by St Peter through a dangerously high sea. In the distance a rainbow and dry land suggest a safe harbour ahead, an appropriate message theologically and politically.

Another visitor to Italy during the time that John Alexander was in Rome was Alexander, Duke of Gordon. As Marquess of Huntly he had fought beside the Earl of Mar at Sheriffmuir against the Duke of Argyll and the Hanoverian army. The Gordons were one of the leading Roman Catholic families in Scotland, with estates in

63

JOHN ALEXANDER

The Rape of Proserpine

Signed and dated: J Alex^r in^t &
pinx^t AD 1720 [JA in monogram]
Oil on canvas
28 x 31$\frac{3}{4}$ (71.1 x 80.7)
National Gallery of Scotland

*The oil sketch for Alexander's most
ambitious work, the twenty-foot-square
staircase ceiling at Gordon Castle, which
has long since disappeared. Alexander's
inspiration for the central section came
from a design by his Roman master
Chiari. The figures of the seasons that fill
the corners probably also have Italian
prototypes, though the source of only one
has been identified: Alexander based his
'Summer' on the figure of Sappho from
the* Parnassus *of Raphael, an artist he
greatly admired.*

Moray and Aberdeenshire. While still a young man the
Marquess had spent some time abroad visiting several of
the great European courts, where he formed friendships
he maintained throughout his life. Cosimo III de'Medici,
Duke of Tuscany, was one such friend; the two dukes
exchanged presents over many years. Foggini's marble
bust of Cosimo III decorated the hall at Gordon Castle.
Cosimo was godfather to Duke Alexander's son, the 3rd
Duke, who was named Cosmo in his honour.

In 1717, two years after his defeat at Sheriffmuir, the
Duke of Gordon was again in Florence visiting the Duke
of Tuscany. He may have met John Alexander then and
even suggested the dedication to Cosimo III of his
Raphael engravings. Contact between the Duke of
Gordon and the artist was to lead to Alexander's greatest
commission, one of the most important decorative projects in Scotland in the eighteenth century, the ceiling
piece for the staircase at Gordon Castle. By 1720 Alexander had completed his oil sketch [*63*], and so similar is it
to Chiari's ceiling of Apollo in the Palazzo Barberini that
it seems likely that Alexander at least received the commission in Italy where he had Chiari's ceiling, the modello for
it, and the artist himself to consult. Alexander's ceiling
shows the abduction of Proserpine in Pluto's chariot. The
scene is framed with a painted cornice, beyond which are
personifications of the four seasons.

Chiari's ceiling, its iconography planned by Bellori, is
more complex than Alexander's. It shows Apollo in his
chariot, rather than Pluto, racing through the skies. A
similar fictive cornice frames the central image; likewise,

64

JOHN ALEXANDER

James, 5th Duke of Hamilton
(1703–43), and the Artist Himself

Signed and dated: J Alex^r hic se
quoque pinxit A D 1724 [JA in
monogram]

Oil on canvas

50 X 40 (127.0 X 101.6)

The Hamilton Collection

figures representing the seasons are fitted into the four corners.

On his return to Scotland, Alexander settled in Edinburgh [64, 67] and had to make a special journey north to Morayshire to paint and install the Rape of Proserpine. He had the task of transferring a small oil sketch to a canvas approximately twenty foot square. He was paid £80, and he also painted three large views of Rome for the castle.

Although based in the south, most of his clients were from the north-eastern counties, and many of them were Jacobites. In 1723 he married Isobel Innes of Tillyfour in Aberdeenshire. Their eldest son, born the following year, was christened Cosmo after the Duke of Gordon's heir. His younger son, Charles, was sent abroad at the age of nine to the Scots Benedictine College at Ratisbon. Duke Cosmo succeeded to the title in 1728 and, like the Grants of Grant, commissioned portraits not only of his family but of his kinsmen and tenants, men like James Gordon of Glastirem, George Gordon of Buckie, David Tulloch of Dumbrenan and the Duke's factor on his

This double portrait of 1724 may have been a gift from the Duke of Hamilton to the Marquess of Annandale. The Duke, his arm resting on a letter addressed to himself, holds a second addressed to the Marquess. It was recorded in the Annandale collection in November 1733 in an inventory compiled by John Alexander himself. The Marquess and the Duke were friends, but why the artist was included in the portrait is not known.

89

65

JOHN ALEXANDER

William, 4th Earl of Kintore
(1702–61)

Oil on canvas
30 x 25 (76.2 x 63.5)
The Kintore Trust

*Alexander's letter to Arthur Gordon of
October 1736 mentions a visit to Keith
Hall during which, from the ages of the
sitters, this and the portrait of William's
sister-in-law Mary could have been
painted.*

66

JOHN ALEXANDER

Mary, Countess of Kintore
(1714–72)

Oil on canvas
30 x 25 (76.2 x 63.5)
The Kintore Trust

*The sitter, the wife of the 3rd Earl of
Kintore, was the daughter of Lord and
Lady Grange. At the time this portrait
was painted, Lady Grange had been kid-
napped by her husband and imprisoned
on St Kilda.*

67
JOHN ALEXANDER

Francis Charteris, later 7th Earl of Wemyss (1723–1808)

Signed and dated: J Alex^r pinx A D 1734 [JA in monogram]
Oil on canvas
52½ x 39¾ (133.3 x 101.0)
The Rt Honble the Earl of Wemyss and March, K.T.

The composition is taken from a mezzotint by Smith after Kneller's portrait of the young Earl of Salisbury, a print which was already almost forty years old when Alexander painted his picture.

Strathbogie estates, John Hamilton, active Jacobites to a man. John Alexander, as the Duke's artist, painted their portraits.

A letter to Arthur Gordon of Carnoussie reveals Alexander's mode of business, how he travelled from house to house in the North-East. Writing in October 1736 from Pitsligo, the home of Lord Forbes, about a portrait of Gordon's wife, the painter first discussed money:

'The price is six guineas, I'm pay'd now that price att Aberdeen, for Pictures of that measure with a hand. Indeed Sir, I have the pleasure, that my payment is the more compleat, in the approbation the Picture has gott, by all your Ladys Friends, that have yet seen it. I made your compliments to my Lord & my Lady Pitsligo, who most heartily return their compliments to you and your Lady. I take my journey tomorrow for Keith Hall [65, 66], so I reckon I shall be att Aberdeen this day eight days, where I'm afraid I might stay a week more, before [I] take

68

WILLIAM MOSMAN

Patrick Duff of Premnay
(1692–1763)

Signed and dated: Gull Mosman
Pingebat 1738

Oil on canvas

29¾ x 24½ (75.6 x 62.2)

Private collection

Two years after Patrick Duff bought Culter House in 1729, Mosman was working as his interior decorator. He painted history pictures for the staircase and created a map room with maps pasted on to the walls for decorative effect. He continued working for Duff in Rome, producing large canvases for the top-floor saloon at Culter (fig. 17). This portrait was painted in 1738, shortly after Mosman returned to Scotland.

journey for Edinburgh: so if there be any thing Sir, that I can serve you, or your Lady in, in the South, you will favour me with your commands, for I really am
    Dear Sir
      Your Most obliged humble Servant
       John Alexander'[22]

By 1736, when this letter was written, William Mosman, fifteen or twenty years younger than John Alexander, was living in Rome. Like the older artist, Mosman was an Aberdonian, an Episcopalian rather than a Roman Catholic, but as a member of a non-juring chapel his sympathies can be presumed to have been Jacobite like Alexander's.

Nothing is known of Mosman's early career until 1727, when, through Sir John Clerk of Penicuik, he had an introduction to William Aikman in London. 'Mr Mosman has been with me,' wrote Aikman to Clerk, 'and I am much afraid he will be of no use to me. I desir'd him to take a lodging near me that I might see him sometimes and I told him I should lett him have pictures to copy. When I see what he can doe I shall be better able to judge what he is

Fig. 16
Culter House by William Mosman. A detail from Mosman's canvas [69] painted for the house

good for and shall doe him all the service lyes in my power.'[23]

Four years later, in the year of Aikman's death, Mosman was working for Patrick Duff, billing him for two history pictures and a portrait.

Patrick Duff of Premnay [68] was one of the many children of Patrick Duff of Craigston in Banffshire. Premnay's uncle was William Duff of Dipple, and two of his first cousins were William Duff of Braco and William, later 1st Earl of Fife.

These Duffs were shrewd bankers who profited from lending money at times of financial difficulty, which in the early eighteenth century were not uncommon in the North-East, with the failure of the Darien Scheme, the South Sea Bubble, the Jacobite forfeitures and several poor harvests. When repayment proved impossible they took over the mortgaged estates themselves. Duff of Premnay acquired Culter House at Peterculter this way [fig. 16]. In the late 1720s he bought up the debts of Sir Alexander Cumin of Culter and the adjoining lands of Drum from the Irvines, drawing accusations of fraud and sharp practice, complaints to which he and his family were well accustomed.

The subjects of the two history pictures which Mosman painted for the staircase at Culter are not known, but in 1736, writing from Italy to Patrick Duff's cousin John Urquhart, he described the main element of a much more ambitious decorative scheme he was painting for Premnay's new house. 'The copy of Aurora for Mr Duff which I finished withal the care I could and I assure you am a considerable loser by it haveing spent above fourteen months on it however hopes it will do the service in the country, meantime if you should be in the country when it arrives I beg you'l be so good as write me your own & other opinions of it for my satisfaction.'[24]

Mosman's copy, after Guido Reni's famous painting in the Casino Rospigliosi, was destined for the ceiling of the saloon at Culter which William Adam had remodelled to replace Alexander Jaffray's earlier room [fig. 17]. Joseph Enzer, who often worked with Adam, was employed to create the plasterwork, and the Norie family probably

93

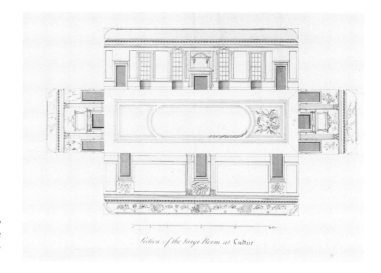

Section of the large Room at Culter

Fig. 17
Design for the saloon at Culter House by William Adam. On loan to Aberdeen University Library. Reproduced by permission of Captain Ramsay of Mar

marbled the pilasters. The saloon is on the second floor of the house, with commanding views of Deeside. Opposite the windows hung a pair of large canvases, also by Mosman; one of these survived the fire of 1910 which destroyed the Aurora and damaged the room. The subject of Erminia carving Tancred's name on a tree is from Tasso, but little of the painting was Mosman's own invention [69]. During his six years in Rome in the 1730s, Mosman studied under Imperiali, and it was one of his master's paintings, now in a private collection in London, that Mosman copied, changing Imperiali's upright into a horizontal by extending the group of animals to the left. As well as changing the composition to fit the space designed by William Adam, Mosman made a further appropriate alteration; he added a view of Culter House to the landscape on the right of the canvas.

While Patrick Duff was commissioning paintings for his new house, the man he described as 'my long, constant and most worthy friend', his cousin Captain John Urquhart, was another of the artist's patrons.

Like the Duke of Gordon, Urquhart, then nineteen, had fought at Sheriffmuir with the Earl of Mar. Subsequently he fled abroad, joined the Spanish navy, was wounded by an English cannonball at the siege of Gibraltar, and became a Roman Catholic. Using some of the considerable profits he had made from privateering, Urquhart was able to buy back for his family his two ancestral castles of Cromarty in the Black Isle and Craigston just north of Turriff. He also embarked on an ambitious spending spree on the Italian art market.

Mosman was his agent, and the two men visited Roman studios together in 1732. Commissions were given, deposits paid, and Mosman remained in the city to see

69
WILLIAM MOSMAN

Erminia Carving Tancred's Name
on a Tree

Oil on canvas
98 x 154½ (248.9 x 392.4)
Private collection

them completed and to organise shipment back to Scotland. Impressed by the young Pompeo Batoni, Urquhart was probably the first foreigner to commission an oil painting from him. This was a full-scale copy of Guido Reni's ceiling of the Ascension in the Vatican, which, after problems with the commission, was installed in Urquhart's house in Aberdeen by March 1735.

The scale of Urquhart's buying was impressive. There were large altarpieces by Trevisani and Imperiali, smaller works by Chiari, Bianchi, Costanzi and Parrocel, in all about fifty works, some copies of famous seventeenth-century paintings, but many originals. As a Jacobite, Urquhart commissioned portraits of the Stewarts. He bought Antonio David's now celebrated pair of Prince Charles and Prince Henry.[25]

Mosman was responsible for despatching these, but, with an eye to a lucrative market in copies, wrote to Urquhart: 'I beg you'l advise me some time befor you give me orders to send off the pictures of P & D [Prince Charles and Prince Henry, Duke of York] because I have begun coppies of them for My Lord Marishal for whom I have to do the K & Q [King and Queen] half length from Trevisani's originals. But, my master willing I should continue drawing this summer from Rafael, have delayed finishing them till winter so if befor that time you incline to have them sent off pray advise me – I shall likewise beg

While Mosman was working in Imperiali's studio in Rome in the mid-1730s, his Italian master was painting an upright picture of Erminia carving her lover Tancred's name on a tree. Mosman copied it and enlarged it on both sides, substantially to the left, to fit a pre-designed space in Patrick Duff's saloon at Culter House. With its pair (now lost), and a ceiling which Mosman copied from Guido Reni, this painting formed the artist's most ambitious decorative scheme.

95

70
WILLIAM MOSMAN
William Duff, Lord Braco (1697–1763), and his son George (born 1736)

Signed and dated: Gul Mosman Pingebat 1741
Oil on canvas
50 x 40 (127.0 x 101.6)
Private collection

This portrait of Lord Braco and his son was painted while William Adam was still at work on Duff House. Relations between architect and client broke down before Adam was able to build the mausoleum to which Lord Braco points in this picture; another mausoleum by a different architect was built later. Its significance to Lord Braco was that it contained memorials of generations of Duffs, a family which claimed descent from the early kings of Scotland.

to know if you design them for Scotland, because if you do I would not spend time here to coppy them for myself presuming you will let me have them to coppy there.'[26]

The following year, in October 1734, Imperiali, a good friend to Scottish artists in Rome, was persuading Mosman to stay on in the city. 'The time of my leaving Rome, as yet I have not altogether determined, my master advising me to resolve upon staying some years longer so as to carry the study of History painting some length, haveing almost finished what is necessary for face painting but, not being in a condition to comply with said advice, must be determined by my friends at home: however resolves after finishing your Magdalene and Mr Duff's Aurora to set about one piece of Invention so that I shall be one & half or two years longer here, notwithstanding it will be with some difficulty.'[27]

Mosman's financial problems were overcome, and he remained in Rome until 1737 or early 1738, for part of the time working alongside a young Edinburgh man, Allan Ramsay, who had joined Imperiali's studio in the winter of 1736–7. He copied Jacobite portraits, painted Erminia and its companion for Culter House, acted as buying and shipping agent for James, the son of Sir John Clerk of Penicuik, and probably undertook further commissions for Patrick Duff and John Urquhart. He also built up his

71
WILLIAM MOSMAN

Jean Grant, Lady Braco (1705–88), and her son Lewis (born 1737)

Signed and dated: Gul Mosman Pingebat 1741
Oil on canvas
50 x 40 (127.0 x 101.6)
Private collection

Lady Braco, a daughter of Sir James Grant of Grant, is painted seated inside Duff House, though in fact, because of her husband's quarrel with the architect, the family never occupied the building. Through the window can be seen to the right William Adam's Fishing Temple on the Deveron. On the top of its dome is a gilded figure of Fame.

own collection of paintings, which he sold in Edinburgh soon after his return.

Mosman was back in Aberdeen in 1738, when he painted three portraits for his patron, Patrick Duff: Duff himself, his wife and his widowed mother-in-law. Three years later, Mosman painted a pair of portraits for Patrick Duff's first cousin, William Duff, Lord Braco (later 1st Earl of Fife), with his son George [70], and Jean, Lady Braco, accompanied by another son, Lewis [71]. Three further portraits of the Braco children were painted in 1741: William, the eldest son, the despair of his father, who had to be restrained by force from joining the Jacobites four years later, James and Alexander, the future 2nd and 3rd Earls of Fife.

Lord Braco, who had employed James Gibbs twenty years earlier to build Balvenie, now needed a larger house for his growing family and ambitions. William Adam was the natural choice to build Duff House, a great palace on the edge of Banff [fig. 18]. It was almost complete in 1741, and as Mosman worked away on the portraits of the children he must have hoped, if not expected, that he would be chosen to decorate it. He was disappointed, for in the same year work stopped on the building when relations between architect and client broke down. A lawsuit followed which was not settled until shortly before

72
WILLIAM MOSMAN

Sir Thomas Kennedy of Culzean, Bt, later 9th Earl of Cassillis (died 1775)

Signed and dated: Gul Mosman Pinxit 1746
Oil on canvas
95 x 58 (241.3 x 147.3)
National Trust for Scotland, Culzean Castle

This portrait, Mosman's most successful large-scale work, was painted in 1746, two years after Sir Thomas had inherited his baronetcy. It is strongly Italianate, an assertion of everything Mosman had learnt during his six years in Rome. The colour scheme is reminiscent of Antonio David, and the nonchalant stance of the young baronet recalls an antique marble such as the Capitoline faun or the poses painted by Mosman's master Imperiali. Even the table looks Italian. Sir Thomas holds a copy of de Vauban's De l'attaque open at plate XIV, showing a design for a fortification.

Fig. 18
Duff House. Engraving by Richard Cooper after William Adam for Vitruvius Scoticus. Reproduced by permission of the Royal Commission on the Ancient and Historical Monuments of Scotland

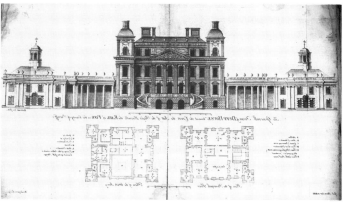

the victorious architect's death in November 1748. Lord Braco is reputed to have refused to set foot in the building, pulling down the blinds of his carriage as he drove past.

For much of the 1740s Mosman was based in Edinburgh. It was there in February 1740, at his house in Writers' Court, that the auction took place of 'a curious collection of *Pictures, Drawings, Statues, Busts, Bass Relievos, Sulphurs*, from intalios and Italian prints belonging to William Mosman . . . collected and done by him during his 6 years residence at Rome, for his own use.'

It was presumably at his studio in Writers' Court during the 1740s that Mosman painted some of the best portraits of his career: Sir Thomas Kennedy of Culzean in 1746 [72], Frances Dunlop in the following year, and the Macdonald Boys, undated but of this period. These portraits show how Roman painting, particularly the soft focus and clear colours of Antonio David and the poses and gestures of Imperiali, continued to influence the artist well after he had left Italy. Mosman finished his career back in his native Aberdeen [73], where, in the early 1760s, he ran a drawing academy. By then his style must have looked very old-fashioned, and the scarcity of dated portraits from the last twenty years of his life leads one to imagine that he may have retired early.

Three other artists who worked in the North-East are worth mentioning. Every one of James Brodie's eight surviving paintings portrays members of his family, and they are datable between 1736 and 1738 [74]. Arresting and distinctive, they are quite unlike any other portraits painted in Britain at that time – in fact their closest parallels are in northern Italy. William Ross is an even

73
WILLIAM MOSMAN

A View of Aberdeen from the South

Oil on canvas
35 x 69 (88.9 x 175.3)
Aberdeen Art Gallery and Museums

Mosman was living in Aberdeen in 1756 when he painted this view of the city for the Town House. It has very obvious faults of perspective, which are surprising from an artist who had studied in Italy for six years. The artist was paid twenty guineas for his work.

74
JAMES BRODIE

Helen Brodie (born 1710)

Signed and dated: Jas Brodie pinxt
1738
Oil on canvas
30 x 25 (76.2 x 63.5)
Messrs Brodies, WS, Edinburgh

*The sitter was almost certainly a close
relation of the artist, possibly his sister.
Her nephew, the son of the cabinet-
maker Francis Brodie, was the infamous
Deacon Brodie.*

75
WILLIAM ROSS

Lewis Rose of Culmoney (dates not
known)

Signed and dated: Wm Ross pinxit
1753
Oil on canvas
30 x 24¾ (76.2 x 62.9)
Miss Elizabeth Rose of Kilravock

*Lewis, or Ludovic, Rose was the son of
Hugh Rose of Kilravock and his wife
Elizabeth Grant of Grant. He merits a
brief description in the family Chronicle:
'Lewis, the second son of the Baron's first
marriage, after feebly attempting to get
into business at Bordeaux, lived for a long
life at Kilravock, as the kind and ready
"Will Wimble", the companion of sport
– the home keeper when others went
abroad – the general man of accounts,
and fact-totum of an indolent family.'*

76
COSMO ALEXANDER
Self-portrait
Oil on canvas
30 x 25⅔ (76.2 x 65.2)
Aberdeen Art Gallery and
Museums

The portrait is not dated, but the youth of the artist suggests it was painted before Alexander was caught up in the events of the '45.

more obscure artist. Only one painting by him is known, a portrait of Lewis Rose of Culmoney dated 1753 [75]. It is a well-observed and engaging portrait, perhaps suggesting a link between Ross and John Alexander.

The Jacobite Rising of 1745 disrupted the career of John and his son Cosmo Alexander, also an artist [76]. They took up arms for Bonnie Prince Charlie and were declared wanted men after the battle of Culloden. John re-emerged earlier than his son, his tightly drawn, angular style softening somewhat as he grew older. It is difficult to tell the difference between the portraits by the father and son in the 1750s or early 1760s unless, like the latter's impressive portrait of the Earl of Fife's factor, James Duff of Corsindae [77], they are signed.

Cosmo made his way to Rome and found business with the Jacobite community in the city. One unusual commission he was keen to secure was the completion of a painting of the battle of Bannockburn which the veteran soldier William Keith, the Earl Marischal, had ordered from Placido Costanzi. The Italian had painted an oil sketch but was having difficulties completing it. Alexander suggested that it would be better finished in Scotland, where the costumes of Robert the Bruce and his soldiers could be more accurately depicted.

77
COSMO ALEXANDER

James Duff of Corsindae
(1678–1762)

Signed and dated: C Alex^r pingebat
AD 1760 [CA in monogram]
Oil on canvas
29¼ x 24¼ (74.3 x 61.6)
National Gallery of Scotland

James Duff bought Corsindae from William Duff, Lord Braco, whose factor he was on Braco's Echt estate, close to Corsindae.

After Rome Cosmo painted briefly in Paris and then settled in Henrietta Street in London, in the furnished house bequeathed to him by his friend and fellow Aberdonian, the architect James Gibbs. He made frequent trips to Scotland, and for two years in 1763 and 1764 worked in Holland, dividing his time between Rotterdam, The Hague and Amsterdam, where his main patrons were a rich business family of Scottish descent, the Hopes [*78*]. In 1766 he sailed to the American colonies, where his sitters were again members of the Scottish community. In Philadelphia he joined the St Andrew's Society (which still exists) and through his contacts painted families like the Rosses and the Ritchies. In 1767 he moved to New York, where again he was elected a member of the local St Andrew's Society. At Newport, Rhode Island, the schoolmaster and doctor Benjamin Waterhouse remembered Cosmo Alexander in his memoirs: 'Mr Alexander associated almost exclusively with the gentlemen from Scotland [and] was said by them to paint for his own amusement. Be that as it may, he soon opened a painting room, well provided with cameras and optical glasses for taking prospective views. He soon put upon canvas the

78
COSMO ALEXANDER
Adrian Hope of Amsterdam
(1709–81)
Signed and dated: C Alex^r pingebat
AD 1763 [CA in monogram]
Oil on canvas
29½ x 24½ (74.9 x 62.2)
National Gallery of Scotland

Hunters, the Keiths, the Fergusons, the Grants, and the Hamiltons.'[28]

Another Scottish family Cosmo Alexander met in Newport was the Stuarts; their fourteen-year-old son Gilbert (later to be famous for his portraits of George Washington) became his assistant and returned with him to Edinburgh in 1771.

Surviving his father by only a few years, Cosmo died in 1772. Father and son had been, pre-eminently, the painters of Scotland's Catholics and Jacobites, and as their numbers diminished through death and conversion – the Gordons had become Protestant in 1728 – Cosmo was forced to travel abroad to find the enclaves of such men and women, whether in Rome or Rhode Island. By 1770 there were few enough of them in Scotland.

The Hopes had left Scotland around 1660 to settle in Holland. Adrian and his brother Thomas founded a bank which became one of the most successful in Europe.

City of Edinburgh

Academies, societies and the patronage of the City of Edinburgh

On 18 October 1729 a group of twenty-eight men met in Edinburgh to sign an agreement. 'We, subscribers, Painters and Lovers of Painting, Fellowes of the Edinburgh School of *St Luke*, for the encouragement of these excelent arts of *Painting, Sculpture, Architecture, etc.*, and Improvement of the Students: Have agreed to erect a publict Academy, wherinto every one that inclines, on aplication to our Director and Council, shal be admitted on paying a smal sum for defraying charges of Figure and lights etc.'[29] The signatories included the two James Nories, father and son, the two Allan Ramsays, poet and painter, John Alexander back from Rome, and the English-born engraver Richard Cooper. Sandy Clerk, Sir John Clerk of Penicuik's brother, the art dealer Andrew Hay, William Adam the architect, and two portrait painters, William Robertson and William Denune, also signed.

The aim of the Academy, named after the famous Roman art school, the Accademia di San Luca, was the improvement of the visual arts in Edinburgh. The old system of trade apprenticeships was no longer sufficient for the aspirations of either the artists listed above or their patrons, men like Lord Linton, Lord Garlies or Sir Gilbert Elliot, who also signed the document.

There were to be two sessions a year, a winter term from November to February and a shorter summer one in June and July. During the winter the Academy would meet for two hours four evenings a week, in the summer for two hours in the early morning, again four days a week. From at least the summer term of 1731, if not from the start, classes were held in a room in the university where students had the opportunity of drawing from the life and copying original works of art, plaster casts, engravings, medals and drawings which had been lent to the Academy.

When Richard Cooper, its first treasurer, moved from London to Edinburgh he brought with him, and put at the Academy's disposal, the fine collection of old master drawings he had acquired abroad. Cooper taught at the

Academy, and one of his pupils, the Orcadian Robert Strange, later gave this description: 'Amongst other advantages to a young artist, we had a winter's academy at Edinburgh. It was superintended by Mr Cooper, who was well qualified for it, and was supported, at the easy subscription of half a guinea, amongst the few artists of that city, and a number of gentlemen who were solicitous of promoting the arts.' Several of the students left the Academy to pursue highly successful careers. Robert Strange himself became one of the finest engravers in Europe, honoured by the academies of Rome, Florence, Bologna, Parma and Paris and knighted by King George III, whose official painter, Allan Ramsay, was another student of the Academy.

Ramsay's sketchbook, produced in the early days of the Academy, survives to give a glimpse of the sort of work done by the students. There are copies after prints by Salvator Rosa, Duquesnoy and François Perrier's scenes of Roman history, the latter copied by the Nories in their decoration at Moray House in the Canongate. Presumably the groups of figures and animals after Nicholas Berchem and architectural arrangements from Panini which occur in the work of the Nories from the 1730s were first seen and sketched in the Academy. How long it survived is not known – possibly until the late 1730s, perhaps even longer.

The Edinburgh Academy of St Luke was one of the first of a number of projects founded to improve the cultural, mercantile and intellectual life of the city during the second quarter of the eighteenth century, when, no longer the capital of a small independent nation, Edinburgh [81] needed to find a new role in the wider context of Great Britain.

In the late 1730s the Earl of Morton and the brilliant young mathematician Colin Maclaurin were jointly responsible for transforming the old Medical Society into the more broadly based Society for Improving Arts and Sciences, to give Scotland an equivalent of the Académie Française and London's Royal Society, of which both men were members. In the new society, founded in 1739 with Maclaurin as secretary and Morton as president, literature and archaeology as well as physics, mathematics and medicine were discussed.

Lord Morton, his wife and five children were painted the following year [79]. The artist was Jeremiah Davison, born in England of Scots parentage. He had met the Duke of Atholl at a Masonic lodge in London, had painted portraits of the Duke and Duchess and had been encouraged to come north. He arrived at the end of 1736, a welcome visitor at a time when, through death or absence

abroad, there were few good portrait painters in Scotland. Indeed, with his fashionable London style, his sophisticated compositions and gleaming satins, Scotland had not seen such an accomplished painter since William Aikman was working in Edinburgh in the early 1720s.

The world of Freemasonry, which had brought Davison and the Duke of Atholl together, was an important forum for social contact in Edinburgh. In 1736 a Grand Lodge of Scotland was formed, and Lord Morton was one of the first Grand Masters. Another prominent Mason, elected Junior Grand Warden in 1738 and in his turn Grand Master, was the celebrated Lord Provost of Edinburgh, George Drummond. It was in 1725 that Drummond began the first of his six two-year terms as Lord Provost, a position of great prestige and patronage of which he made full and beneficial use. More than any other individual, Drummond was concerned with improving the status and fabric of the city and university, the latter then under the control of the Town Council. With George Drummond as Lord Provost, new faculties were created and the ablest

79
JEREMIAH DAVISON

James, 13th Earl of Morton and his family

Signed and dated: J Davison pinxit 1740
Oil on canvas
95 x 112⅛ (241.3 x 284.7)
Scottish National Portrait Gallery

Lord Morton commissioned this portrait in 1740 for his new house at Dalmahoy, a few miles west of Edinburgh. The Earl played a significant part in the intellectual life of the city, and was also president of the Royal Society, a member of the Académie Française, and one of the first Trustees of the British Museum.

80

JOHN ALEXANDER

George Drummond (1687–1766)

Signed and dated: J Alex^r pin (x^t)

AD 1752 [JA in monogram]

Oil on canvas

49½ x 40 (125.7 x 101.6)

Royal Infirmary of Edinburgh

George Drummond was the single most important citizen of Edinburgh during the eighteenth century; few of the civic improvements of the age were not the product of his vision and determination. The sash window in this portrait has been raised to reveal one of his projects, the Royal Infirmary, which when the picture was painted had recently been completed to the design of William Adam.

men appointed professors. The Royal Exchange was built, the Nor' Loch drained and the New Town planned, but the greatest project of Drummond's career, which he saw through from beginning to end, was the foundation of a Royal Infirmary, housed in the building by William Adam which appears in the background of his portrait by John Alexander [*80*].

Like many of Drummond's improvements, the Infirmary had its origins in the 1680s, when, during James, Duke of York's residence at Holyroodhouse, the Royal College of Physicians was founded. In 1725, the physicians called a public meeting to appeal for funds to set up a teaching hospital. They were impressed by the medical schools of Holland, and of Leiden in particular, where many of them had trained and where theoretical and practical teaching were combined. So great was the response to the physicians' appeal that a small house in Robertson's Close was converted and soon plans were laid and William Adam employed to build a much larger, more ambitious hospital. The subsequent appeal generated unprecedented support, with money raised from all corners of Scotland, Scottish communities overseas and elsewhere. The

creation of the Infirmary was rightly and proudly seen as a great national project. 'I take it for granted', wrote a contemporary, 'You are by this time persuaded that no Hospital in Europe is so well served in physicians and surgeons, either for number or eminence as this one has the prospect of being.'[30]

In 1740 the foundation stone of the west wing was laid by the Grand Master Mason, the Earl of Morton. The east wing, under construction, was opened the following year, to be converted into a military hospital during the Jacobite Rising four years later. By the end of the decade the hospital was at last complete. At its centre, professionally and geographically, behind William Adam's grand front-ispiece, was the theatre, designed to hold two hundred students. As the patient lay on the operating table he would have looked up to heaven and seen John Alexander's decoration of the cupola, copied from Raphael's Chigi Chapel ceiling in S. Maria del Popolo in Rome, showing God the father surrounded by symbols of the planets.

While the creation of the Royal Infirmary helped to establish Edinburgh's reputation for medical excellence, the foundation of the Royal Bank of Scotland in 1727 assisted the city's development as a financial centre. The 2nd Duke of Argyll's brother, the able Lord Ilay, was the first Governor, and, with his agent Andrew Fletcher, Lord Milton [82], and Lord Provost George Drummond as two of the nine ordinary directors, the Royal Bank introduced a new system of cash credits, greatly encouraging business investment.

Early in the Bank's history, from at least 1732, John Campbell (known to the Gaelic world as Iain Caimbeul a'bhanca – John Campbell of the Bank) was at first

81
WILLIAM DELACOUR
Edinburgh from the East
Signed and dated: Delacour px
1759
Oil on canvas
42½ x 90¼ (108.0 x 229.2)
City of Edinburgh Art Centre

This accurate and detailed view of the city from Spring Gardens, probably drawn with the aid of a camera obscura, belonged to the amateur artist John Clerk of Eldin in the eighteenth century. Clerk's friend, the topographical draughtsman Paul Sandby, whose work Clerk owned, had drawn the city and its street life a few years before Delacour arrived in Edinburgh [fig. 19, p.116]. It is possible that this panorama, unique in Delacour's work, was prompted by Sandby's drawings of the city.

82

ALLAN RAMSAY

Andrew Fletcher, Lord Milton
(1692–1766)

Signed and dated: A Ramsay, 1748
Oil on canvas
29⅞ x 24⅞ (76.0 x 63.2)
J.T.T. Fletcher of Saltoun

Lord Milton was the 3rd Duke of Argyll's confidential agent, skilfully managing Scottish politics in the Argyll interest. He resigned his office of Lord Justice General the year this portrait was painted.

Assistant Secretary and from 1745 Cashier, responsible to the governor and directors for its day-to-day business. It was Campbell who on 14 September 1745, knowing that Edinburgh would soon be in the control of the Jacobites, closed the bank in the High Street and moved its assets up the Royal Mile to the safety of the Castle. Four years later he was painted by William Mosman, standing at a table on which lies one of his bank notes [*83*]. Campbell, rather than Mosman, dictated the detailed iconography of the portrait, which reveals several of his many interests. First and foremost was his pride of birth. John Campbell was descended from the head of the house of Argyll, the family of the Governor, Lord Ilay, who by 1759, when Campbell wrote Lord Milton the following letter, had succeeded his brother as 3rd Duke of Argyll and Chieftain of the Clan [*101*]: 'Clanish as my attatchments may be to any thing relating to the family of my chief, yet when I thought on the firm and steady friendship that has so long subsisted between the present head of it and your Lordship, I could not forbear sending you the picture of the first Duke, which I lately, very casually mentioned to be in my possession.

83
WILLIAM MOSMAN
John Campbell of the Bank
(died 1777)

Oil on canvas
46½ x 56⅔ (118.0 x 144.0)
The Royal Bank of Scotland plc

'Trifling as this present may be, some reason I had for placing it in my little collection, when I take the liberty to tell your Lordship (as a friend) that the person from whom I have my descent stood in the same degree of relation to the Marquis of Argyll as did the Duke whose portrait I now send.'[31]

John Campbell was the great-grandson of the Marquis of Argyll [2] and the second cousin of the 3rd Duke. His father was the 1st Earl of Breadalbane's son, Colin Campbell of Ardmaddy, and it is Ardmaddy Bay, with its three rocks pointing out to Seil Sound, which Mosman depicted in the background of the portrait. Just visible too is the cave in the cliff where Neil Campbell of Ardmaddy had hidden in times of danger. The window in the painting provides a view of John Campbell's ancestral territory and history. His very elaborate and traditional Highland dress of the belted plaid, decorated cross-belt, targe and weapons recall his status as a senior member of his clan.

His confidence in wearing Highland dress only two years after it had been proscribed by Act of Parliament indicates his secure position as a trusted Hanoverian in a prominent

The date 1771 inscribed on the painting is the year Campbell died, not the date of the portrait; that is indicated on the banknote, signed by him, as April 1749. It is an indication of Campbell's confidence as a trusted establishment figure that he chose to be portrayed in Highland dress so soon after its proscription. [Reproduced in colour as the frontispiece.]

Whig clan. Campbell was successful in straddling the two worlds of Gaelic society and Lowland commerce; he was admired for this and celebrated by the poet Duncan Ban Macintyre. Even the marble-topped table, although present in some other Mosman paintings, may have its significance in the portrait. Campbell had a financial interest in the Netherlorn marble quarries near Ard-maddy. He also had a factory at Leith docks which made such tables, one of which he presented to Lord Milton.

Mosman was one of several painters working in Edinburgh during the late 1740s and 1750s [*84*]. Some, like John Alexander or William Denune [*86, 88*], although based in the city, had built up a clientele in other parts of Scotland, in Alexander's case in the North-East, in Denune's, Dumfriesshire. Allan Ramsay had his main operation in London but spent a few months most years painting portraits in Edinburgh [*87, 89*]. Philip Mercier from York was in the city in 1750. Towards the end of that decade William Millar was beginning to build up a portrait practice [*85*].

Something resembling an art market was beginning to develop in the capital, with resident picture dealers like William Murray and David Nevay. Auctions of paintings, prints and sculpture were more common than they had been earlier in the century, and the lots were better described. John Esplen and Charles Robertson were auctioneers, both combining this with selling artists' materials, Robertson running a decorative painting business as well. But the leaders in that field were still the Nories; their large, well-organised firm secured, amongst much other business, the lucrative government contracts to work at the garrisons at Fort Augustus, Fort William and Edinburgh Castle. These fortresses were being repaired and strengthened following the recent rebellion.

Another part of the government's anti-Jacobite programme, to remedy its lack of knowledge of the geography of Scotland, was the preparation of an accurate and detailed map of the country. This was produced by surveying parties in the field reporting back to the Board of Ordnance headquarters at Edinburgh Castle. Paul Sandby was the official draughtsman, and although his job took him all over Scotland most of his time was probably spent in the capital, where he became part of the intellectual circle centred on the Ramsays, the Adams, who had the contract for rebuilding the Highland forts, and John Clerk of Eldin, Sir John Clerk of Penicuik's talented son. Sandby sketched the life of the city [fig. 19] on the eve of the development of the New Town, when the upper and lower classes still shared the same overcrowded tenements, standing many stories high above the High Street

84

WILLIAM MOSMAN

James Stuart (died 1777)

Signed and dated: Gul Mosman
pingebat 1740
Oil on canvas
33½ x 28 (85.0 x 71.1)
City of Edinburgh Art Centre

*James Stuart's name, and his occupation
as an Edinburgh merchant, are revealed
on the letter he holds in his hand. The
ledger and ink-stand are illustrative of
his profession. Over twenty years after
this portrait was painted, Stuart succeeded George Drummond as Lord Provost of Edinburgh after Drummond's
final term of office. The portrait of
Stuart's wife, Elizabeth, also painted by
Mosman in 1740, possibly at the time of
their marriage, is in the National Gallery of Scotland.*

85

WILLIAM MILLAR

Thomas Trotter (born 1682)

Oil on canvas
29 x 24½ (73.7 x 62.2)
National Gallery of Scotland

Trotter holds a copy of the Caledonian
Mercury. *It was published three times a
week; Thomas Ruddiman [86] was its
owner and publisher for much of the
century.*

113

86

WILLIAM DENUNE

Thomas Ruddiman (1674–1757)

Signed and dated: De Nune pinx
1749
Oil on canvas
29⅛ x 25⅛ (74.0 x 63.8)
Scottish National Portrait Gallery

Thomas Ruddiman was a printer and publisher, the owner of the Caledonian Mercury *newspaper. From 1730, until he was succeeded by David Hume in 1752, Ruddiman was also the Keeper of the Advocates' Library.*

87

ALLAN RAMSAY

Sir John Inglis of Cramond, Bt
(1683–1771)
Oil on canvas
30 x 25 (76.2 x 63.5)
National Gallery of Scotland

Sir John was probably painted in the mid-1740s, when he held the position of Post Master General of Scotland. In 1736, at the celebrated trial of John Porteous, Inglis was Chancellor of the Jury; Lord Milton [82] was the judge.

88

WILLIAM DENUNE

Anne Smith, Mrs Ruddiman
(died 1769)

Signed and dated: De Nune pinx
1749
Oil on canvas
30 x 25$\frac{1}{16}$ (76.2 x 63.7)
Scottish National Portrait Gallery

89

ALLAN RAMSAY

Anne Cockburn, Lady Inglis
(dates not known)

Oil on canvas
30 x 25 (76.2 x 63.5)
National Gallery of Scotland

*Both Lady Inglis and her husband are
likely to have been painted in Edinburgh,
where Ramsay usually tried to spend a
few months of each year during the 1740s
and early 1750s.*

Fig. 19
An entertainment in the grounds of Heriot's Hospital, Edinburgh, by Paul Sandby. Reproduced by Gracious Permission of Her Majesty The Queen

and Cowgate. Sandby was the first artist to illustrate Ramsay's *Gentle Shepherd*, his etchings inspiring John Clerk of Eldin. His watercolour landscapes and genre scenes influenced those of Alexander Runciman and David Allan.

In 1754, shortly after Sandby had moved back to London, Allan Ramsay, who had spent much of that year in Edinburgh, founded the Select Society, whose purpose was conversation and debate. By any standards its membership was impressive. David Hume and Adam Smith were co-founders with Ramsay, and as the society's prestige grew, so did the pressure to increase the membership, limited initially to fifty. As Hume remarked, 'It has grown to be a National Concern. Young and old, noble and ignoble, witty and dull, laity and clergy, all the world are ambitious of a place amongst us, and on each occasion we are as much solicited by candidates as if we were to choose a Member of Parliament.'

Hume was painted the year the society was founded [90]. Even by the high standards of Ramsay's portraits of this period, it is exceptional. Hume's was not an easy head to paint. 'Nature,' wrote a contemporary, 'never formed a man more unlike his real character . . . His face was broad and fat, his mouth wide, and without any other expression than that of imbecility.'[32] Yet Ramsay's portrait reveals the true intelligence and humour of the great philosopher and historian, while depicting, most beautifully, his physical appearance as well.

As Ramsay and Hume's Select Society was established for the benefit of Edinburgh's intelligentsia, in the same year, 1754, the Edinburgh Society for Encouraging Arts, Sciences, Manufactures, and Agriculture was founded for its artisans; 'that the inhabitants of Scotland might

90
ALLAN RAMSAY
David Hume (1711–76)
Signed and dated: A Ramsay 1754
Oil on canvas
30 x 25 (76.2 x 63.5)
Private collection

Hume, one of the greatest European philosophers, was a good friend of the artist.

become diligent in labour and excellent in arts, were the purposes for which the Edinburgh Society was instituted – purposes, in which all who love their country are, and must be, deeply interested. To attain these, a proper distribution of premiums, seemed the way most reasonable and probable. The good effects of this method in Ireland, gave the highest encouragement to attempt it here.'

In its annual art competitions, open to boys under twenty, prizes were awarded for the best drawings of sculpture, architecture, landscape or foliage. Entrants were not allowed to invent their compositions but must copy from paintings, sculpture, prints or drawings. The purpose of the competitions was to improve the quality of design of manufactured goods, the same reason that in 1760 an academy was established in Edinburgh by the Board of Trustees for Fisheries, Manufactures and Improvements in Scotland. The Trustees Academy was the first design school in Britain.

Lord Milton, Lord Belhaven and George Drummond [*82, 40, 80*] were three of the Trustees of the Board of Manufactures, as it became known. It may have been Lord

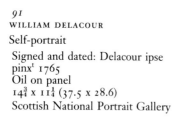

91
WILLIAM DELACOUR

Self-portrait

Signed and dated: Delacour ipse
pinx^t 1765
Oil on panel
14¾ x 11¼ (37.5 x 28.6)
Scottish National Portrait Gallery

Milton's influence that secured the job of first Master of
the Trustees Academy for the Frenchman William Delacour [*91*], for Delacour had already decorated Lord
Milton's house in the Canongate. That commission had
not been entirely without its problems. John Adam, who
was the architect of Milton House, acted as a middleman
between Delacour and his patron. 'Mr Delacour is pro-
ceeding with your Lordship's room according to the
design formerly approved of by your Lordship, and so far
as it is yet come, it promises extremely well. But as I was
afraid he might be going further than your Lordship
would incline, I desired him to make out an estimate of the
whole expense, to finish it in the genteelest taste, and so as
to keep every part in harmony, that I might transmit it to
your Lordship for directions. The arabesque painting and
landskips he desired me formerly to acquaint your Lordship, would be about 35 or £36 besides the plain painting
of the room. This he still agrees to, and says he could not
afford it so low to any other body, as he wants by this to
introduce himself to business. I told him your Lordship
was so good as say, you would keep his secret, and that he
ought therefor to exert himself, which he has promised . . .
He has done one door with party gilding, which indeed
has an excessive fine effect, and Mr Ramsay who saw it
before his departure for London, was highly pleas'd with

92

WILLIAM DELACOUR

Three Decorative Landscapes

Oil on plaster
The uprights 63¼ x 41½
(160.7 x 105.4)
The horizontal 50½ x 55¾
(128.3 x 141.6)
University of Edinburgh

These three landscapes were part of a scheme of decoration commissioned by Sir Thomas Miller, Lord Glenlee, for his house in Brown Square, Edinburgh. In 1759 Miller succeeded Andrew Pringle, Lord Alemoor, as Solicitor General. Pringle was also a patron of Delacour, who painted oval canvases for his villa, Hawkhill, on the edge of Edinburgh.

Fig. 20
The saloon at Yester. The photograph shows some of the paintings by William Delacour which decorate the Adam room

it, as he was with the whole design, after he saw it sketch'd in upon the walls; But I have desired Mr Delacour not to run further into gilding till your Lordships pleasure is known. I am very much convinced that if your Lordship does allow him to go on according to his intention, that it will give satisfaction, and will make the finest room by much, that we have in this countrey.'[33]

It was as well that John Adam had written, for Lord Milton was furious that the artist had gone beyond what had been agreed. The elaborate gilding which Ramsay and Adam had so much admired was scrapped.

Delacour's arrival in Edinburgh coincided with the death of James Norie in June 1757. Robert Norie, now running the firm, was not the equal of his father, and it was Delacour who secured the commissions to decorate the interiors of the houses and villas built by John and Robert Adam, who were running the company after their father's death [92].

Lord Alemoor's suburban villa, Hawkhill, was one such collaboration. Much more ambitious was their partnership at Yester. There, in the saloon on the first floor, working on a large scale with seven ten-foot-high canvases of classical ruins and landscapes, William Delacour and Robert and William Adam created one of the loveliest rooms in Scotland [fig. 20]. Delacour's ability to work on such a scale was due to the experience he had gained in the theatre; indeed it may have been a job as a scene painter that brought him to Scotland in the first place [93]. In 1757 he painted a wood scene for Hume's *Douglas*. Two years later he was paid for his work on Voltaire's *Orphan of China* with a benefit performance on the third night. Other sets were painted for the theatre in Glasgow as well

as Edinburgh, until in 1763 he was dismissed by both managements after a row about payment.

By then he had been running the Trustees Academy for three years, earning a regular income from the two separate classes he supervised. The first, for which he was paid quarterly by the Trustees, was to teach industrial design, particularly the drawing of patterns for linen and woollen goods. Applicants for this course were selected by the Board of Trustees. For a guinea a quarter, anyone was able to join Delacour's fine-art class, women as well as men, though they were taught separately.

The Academy of the Board of Manufactures had a long and distinguished history. It prospered under Delacour, who was a talented and successful teacher. Later in the century its masters included Alexander Runciman and David Allan. Like many of the new initiatives which were begun in mid-eighteenth-century Scotland, the Trustees Academy, the Royal Bank and the Royal Infirmary fulfilled the hopes of the men like Lord Morton, Lord Milton and Provost Drummond, whose creations they were.

93
WILLIAM DELACOUR

Capriccio Landscape

Signed and dated: Delacour 1756
Oil on canvas
43½ x 51¼ (110.5 x 130.2)
Private collection

Painted in 1756, close to the time that the artist settled in Edinburgh, this imaginary landscape probably has similarities with the backcloths and sets Delacour produced for the theatre.

Bute

Allan Ramsay and the patronage of John, 3rd Earl of Bute

John Stuart and Allan Ramsay were born in Edinburgh in the same year. Each inherited advantages that enabled him to reach the summit of his chosen career. John Stuart, the son and heir of the Earl of Bute and nephew of John, 2nd Duke of Argyll, made politics his profession. Art was Allan Ramsay's pursuit.

John Stuart's advantages were of birth, education and connection. So too were Ramsay's. Though he did not belong to the same aristocratic world of the Butes and Argylls, his father, the poet Allan Ramsay [56], and his father's friends formed an intellectual aristocracy in Edinburgh which had contacts far beyond the city. The young Ramsay's connections were the writers, collectors and philosophers of Europe. It was they who were useful in his progress as a painter.

At every stage in his career Allan Ramsay was able to make use of the network of connections that his father had made in the world of art and literature. In 1734, when he was in London for the first time, studying under Hans Hysing and drawing from the life at the St Martin's Lane Academy, the young painter's teacher was William Hogarth, whose engravings of *Hudibras* had been dedicated to his father. A year later Ramsay senior took up his pen on his son's behalf to solicit and cajole the Lord Provost of Edinburgh to support his scheme for sending his son abroad. In May 1736 he was able to write of his success to his friend John Smibert in Boston: 'Allan has been pursuing your science since he was a dozen years auld – was with Mr Hyssing, at London, for some time about two years ago: has been since at home, painting here like a Raphael – set out for the seat of the Beast, beyond the Alps, within a month hence – to be away about two years. – I'm sweer to part with him, but canna stem the current, which flows from the advice of his patrons, and his own inclinations.'

Ramsay travelled abroad with Alexander Cunyngham, one of the Cunynghams of Caprington near Kilmarnock.

He took with him an introduction to Pierre-Jean Mariette, the great Parisian connoisseur and collector who, in his turn, provided further contacts for the artist in Italy. Ramsay's choice of master there is likely to have been determined before he left Edinburgh. Imperiali, who was teaching William Mosman at the time Ramsay joined his studio, was the artist best known and most favoured in Scotland. But it was Mariette's letters which unlocked the doors of the Palazzo Mancini, home of the excellent French Academy in Rome, run at the time of Ramsay's arrival by Nicolas Wleughels. Ramsay wrote to thank Mariette for his help: 'As soon as we arrived in Rome we immediately availed ourselves of the introduction which you had the kindness to give us to the Director of the French Academy; and here, as previously in Florence, we discovered what it means to be recommended by persons of worth and discernment.'[34]

From Rome Ramsay moved south to Naples, where, thanks to the influence of a friend of his father, he had the distinction of being the only Briton to be taught by the doyen of Italian painting, Francesco Solimena. Despite having turned eighty Solimena's abilities had not decreased with age – if anything the reverse was true. His work, while Ramsay was in his studio, was vigorous, dramatic and richly coloured. The influence of Solimena and the Franco-Roman painter Pierre Subleyras, much more than Imperiali, can be seen in the only painting known to date from Ramsay's first Italian period, the portrait of his friend Samuel Torriano, a member of a distinguished and well-connected Anglo-Italian family.

When Ramsay returned to Britain during the summer of 1738, he was not yet twenty-five. He had already enjoyed exceptional opportunities for travel and study in sophisticated and cosmopolitan company, which none of his English rivals had at his age begun to experience. At twenty-four, Hogarth, for instance, had hardly served his long apprenticeship as an engraver, or been out of London, and Reynolds, closer to Ramsay in age, was still a humble West-Country portrait painter.

Before Ramsay left for Italy he had become engaged to Anne Bayne. Her father was the Professor of Scots Law at the University of Edinburgh; her mother was a grand-daughter of the architect Sir William Bruce. Ramsay painted two portraits of Anne, one possibly before their engagement [94], the other probably at the time of their marriage, when Ramsay painted a companion self-portrait [95]. The first portrait of Anne, hardly more than a girl, is Ramsay's early masterpiece – far superior to, but still a product of, the rather narrow world of William Denune and other provincial Scottish artists. Between the time

94
ALLAN RAMSAY

Anne Bayne (died 1743)

Oil on canvas
27 x 21 (68.6 x 53.3)
Scottish National Portrait Gallery

Ramsay married his first wife in 1739, less than a year after returning from his first visit to Italy. This portrait may pre-date both his journey and engagement.

95
ALLAN RAMSAY

Self-portrait

Oil on canvas
24 x 18¼ (61.0 x 46.4)
National Portrait Gallery, London

when the first and second portraits of Anne were painted she had become a woman, no longer demure but poised, witty rather than timid. No doubt she had grown up during the three or four years that separate these portraits, but it was really the painter who had changed. Ramsay had returned from Italy transformed from a talented and promising provincial to the best and most sophisticated portrait painter in Great Britain.

Like Aikman twenty years before, and for the same reasons, Ramsay settled in London. He opened a studio in Covent Garden, and his success was immediate. One of the first men to sit to him was in fact Aikman's old patron John, Duke of Argyll, and it is hard not to believe that the reason the sixty-year-old Duke sat to Ramsay was to give public support to a young Scottish artist in order to encourage others to do the same. The Duke sat during the winter of 1739–40, and with his permission a mezzotint of the portrait was prepared which was advertised first in the *Caledonian Mercury* of 7 February 1740. 'Speedily will be published a whole length print of his Grace the Duke of Argyle in the robes of the Garter, by Mr Faber, from an original picture by Allan Ramsay Junior: who ever inclines to secure copies of the first impressions, let them notify their demands to Allan Ramsay Senior in Edinburgh, and their commissions shall be taken care of.' The father was still actively and proudly promoting his son, even providing a studio in his new house on Castle Hill where the painter could work on his regular visits back to Edinburgh. The father could be useful in London too. He had been a correspondent of the eminent doctor Richard Mead, who had treated both Watteau and Aikman for tuberculosis and had formed a remarkable collection of contemporary international art, including work by Scottish painters. Ramsay's grand full-length of Mead, Neapolitan in its rich colouring, individual in its honest characterisation, was presented to the Foundling Hospital, the charity dear to the hearts of Hogarth and Handel, where it was publicly seen and admired.

The portrait of Mead, like the portrait of the 2nd Duke of Argyll, was engraved, helping to spread Ramsay's growing reputation. In 1744, the year after the death of his elder brother, Archibald Campbell, the Earl of Ilay, now 3rd Duke of Argyll, also sat to Ramsay, and Faber again engraved the portrait.

The two Dukes of Argyll had a sister, Lady Anne, who was the mother of John Stuart, 3rd Earl of Bute. The father had died when his eldest son was only ten, and the young Earl had been brought up in the houses of his Campbell uncles. The Earl's younger brother James married one of his cousins, and the two families, the Butes and

96
ALLAN RAMSAY
Lady Mary Campbell, Viscountess
Coke (1726–1811)

Oil on canvas
91 X 57 (231.1 X 144.8)
Private collection

the Argylls, could hardly have been closer [*96*]. In 1736 John, 3rd Earl of Bute, eloped with and married Mary Wortley Montagu; and the couple spent the first decade of their married life back in Scotland, living on the island of Bute, the Earl playing his part in Scottish affairs, studying architecture, agriculture and botany and running his estates. In 1745 the Butes were back in London, living in Twickenham. Lady Bute's mother, the eccentric Lady Mary Wortley Montagu, explained why: 'As regards Lord Bute and my daughter's coming to Town, it may be owing to the advice of the Duke of Argyle. It was a maxim of Sir R. Walpole's that whoever expected advancement should

The unhappy marriage of Lord Bute's first cousin, Lady Mary Campbell, and the heir of the Earl of Leicester, Viscount Coke, ended, after separation, in his early death. Ramsay painted her twice in her widowhood: first in 1758 and then four years later, in this most elegant of all his female full-lengths. Lady Mary holds a theorbo, a musical instrument which she had borrowed from her friend Lady Ancram and had refused to return.

127

97
ALLAN RAMSAY

John, 3rd Earl of Bute (1713–92)

Signed or inscribed: Ramsay pinxit
1758
Oil on canvas
94¼ x 57⅞ (239.4 x 147.0)
National Trust for Scotland, Bute
House

The head and shoulders of the sitter were painted on a small canvas which was then enlarged to the present size. A recent cleaning has removed a very discoloured varnish and revealed the delicacy and subtlety of Ramsay's paint throughout. The long inscription states that this was the original portrait painted for the Prince of Wales. A version wholly autograph, of very high quality, was painted for Lord Bute and has remained in the possession of the family.

appear much in public. He used to say, whoever neglected the world would be neglected by it, tho' I believe more families have been ruined by that method than raised by it.'[35] Two years later the advice paid off. Frederick, Prince of Wales, the eldest son of George II, was at Cliveden watching a cricket match. During the course of the game it started to rain and play was suspended. As the royal party needed to be kept amused, an equerry suggested whist, and Lord Bute was asked to make up a fourth.

The handsome, intelligent and lively Butes soon became members of the Prince of Wales's set, based at Leicester House, the home of Frederick and Augusta of Wales, which was the centre of political opposition to the King. In

98
ALLAN RAMSAY
Margaret Lindsay (died 1782)
Oil on canvas
30 x 25 (76.2 x 63.5)
National Gallery of Scotland

1750 Lord Bute was made a Lord of the Bedchamber and the following year Groom of the Stole. The unexpected death of Frederick, Prince of Wales, in 1751 did nothing to harm his position. Without a husband Princess Augusta relied increasingly on Lord Bute, who became the tutor of her son George and the intimate friend of them both.

Ramsay's wife Anne died in 1743, and it was some time before he remarried. His second wife was Margaret Lindsay [98], a niece of Lord Mansfield, the Lord Chancellor of England. Her family, the Lindsays of Evelick, disapproved of the match, and the couple, like the Butes, eloped. The marriage took place in Edinburgh in March 1752. Some time towards the end of the following year Ramsay left London. It had been his practice for some time to spend several months of the year in Scotland, painting in his father's house and seeing his family and friends. On this occasion, whether or not it was his intention on starting, he was to be away from London for four years. The first was spent in Edinburgh, the three subsequent years in Italy. It is usually claimed that it was the arrival of Joshua Reynolds from Rome during the winter of 1752–3 which precipitated Ramsay's absence.

This portrait of his second wife is one of the most celebrated of all Ramsay's portraits, one that could easily have inspired Horace Walpole's remark: 'Mr Reynolds and Mr Ramsay can scarce be rivals; their manners are so different. The former is bold, and has a kind of tempestuous colouring, yet with dignity and grace; the latter is all delicacy. Mr Reynolds seldom succeeds in women: Mr Ramsay is formed to paint them.'

99
DAVID MARTIN
Robert Adam (1728–92)
Oil on canvas
50 x 40 (127.0 x 101.6)
National Portrait Gallery, London

When Adam was in Rome in the mid-1750s he and Allan Ramsay sketched the classical ruins of the city. Later they were both employed by Lord Bute, Adam designing Luton Hoo and what is now called Lansdowne House in Berkeley Square. This portrait may be by Ramsay's assistant David Martin. Adam appears to be seated in Martin's studio chair.

Certainly Reynolds's newly acquired abilities must have surprised any observer used to his earlier provincial style. Like Ramsay in 1738 Reynolds had returned a mature artist, with his own personal, confident and forceful style. But Ramsay's decision to absent himself from London must have been taken before the younger artist had achieved his full success. None of the forty or so portraits which Ramsay painted in Edinburgh from the winter of 1753 to midsummer 1754 show any recognition of the Venetian colouring and liveliness of Reynolds's recent work: quite the reverse is true of his finest paintings of that period. The portraits of David Hume [*90*] or Lord Drummore, for example, show Ramsay moving in the opposite direction; restraint rather than passion is the characteristic of these acutely observed portraits.

Ramsay had been painting in London with great success but without a break for fifteen years. It seems more likely that he made his decision to travel for personal reasons. In October 1752 Margaret Ramsay bore twins who died only hours after their birth. In the last week of 1753 Ramsay received a greater blow in the death of his 'much accomplished' ten-year-old daughter Anne. She was the last remaining child of his first marriage, and for the first time in thirteen years Ramsay was left without children. He was a successful man with money to spend. He had a pretty wife who had never travelled. He would have heard from his friends, the Adams, that Robert was setting out for Rome at the end of 1754 with Charles Hope. Robert Wood, the classical scholar and a friend, was already in Italy. It is not surprising, therefore, that the Ramsays also decided to go. They were in Florence in October and in Rome by March the following year, living on the Viminale, slightly out of the fashionable centre where Robert Adam [99] was intent on cutting a figure.

Ramsay was hard at work, painting a few portraits, but spending most of his time drawing. He had always been an exceptionally gifted draughtsman. At the age of sixteen he drew a portrait of his father which the latter presented to Sir Gilbert Elliot of Minto at the time of the establishment of the Academy of St Luke. He had drawn in Rome on his first visit, both in the studio of Imperiali and at the French Academy; and it was to the Academy, now run by Natoire, himself an exquisite draughtsman, that Ramsay returned. He also frequented the studio of Batoni, an artist who had appealed to him in the thirties. Twenty years later Batoni had become the leading Italian portrait painter, rivalled but not equalled by Anton Rafael Mengs. Perhaps in emulation of Natoire and his students, who were sent out from the French Academy to draw the Roman landscape, Robert Adam, his French drawing master Clérisseau, and Ramsay went out on similar sketching expeditions.

The young and irrepressible Adam, intoxicated by Rome, could get exasperated by Ramsay's steady middle-aged ways; but he admitted in his letters home that the company of the Ramsays and their frequent comings and goings made Roman life agreeable. There was in fact quite a circle of friends in Rome, including Robert Wood and the Abbé Grant, the Scottish Catholic agent in Rome, both of whom Ramsay painted at this time. David Martin, Ramsay's eighteen-year-old assistant, joined them in 1755 to draw and paint, until May 1757, when Adam and Clérisseau in one coach and the Ramsays in a second left Rome to return to Britain.

The Ramsays were back in London by August 1757. The old house and studio in Covent Garden were sold and they moved fashionably west to Soho Square. Within a couple of months Ramsay received the most important commission of his career to date, a full-length portrait of George, Prince of Wales, the nineteen-year-old heir to the throne [100]. The commission was due to Lord Bute, the Prince's tutor and close friend. Although the Earl himself had

100
ALLAN RAMSAY
George III as Prince of Wales
(1738–1820)

Oil on canvas
93 x 58 (236.2 x 147.3)
Private collection

The success of this portrait gained Ramsay royal approval and patronage, which raised him above his contemporaries and made him a very rich man. When Lord Eglinton suggested that George III might sit to Reynolds, the King brusquely remarked: 'Mr Ramsay is my painter, my Lord.'

never previously employed Ramsay, he had followed the lead of his Campbell uncles, sitting to Aikman in his youth and now selecting the artist they had continuously supported [*101*]. The suggestion of Ramsay as the artist to paint the Prince was certainly Lord Bute's, but whether the commission came from him or the Prince is not known: it was probably the Earl's, whose influence was very great. What appears to be a reciprocal commission of the Earl by Ramsay was commanded by the Prince shortly after.

Ramsay was at work at Kew by October, making preliminary drawings. For a pose he used a classical source that he

101
ALLAN RAMSAY

Archibald, 3rd Duke of Argyll
(1682–1761)

Signed and dated: A Ramsay 1758
Oil on canvas
49 x 39 (124.5 x 99.1)
His Grace The Duke of
Northumberland

had seen in Rome, the Hermes Farnese in the Vatican Belvedere. He had already turned to classical sculpture for inspiration ten years earlier when he had chosen the Belvedere's more famous Apollo for his pose for the Macleod of Macleod, a source which later also appealed to Reynolds. When Ramsay was considering the Prince's portrait he was able to recall how Batoni had used the Hermes Farnese for his first royal commission, the portrait of the young Karl Eugen, Duke of Württemberg, an exact contemporary of the Prince of Wales. Batoni's portrait of the Duke was in his studio when Ramsay was sketching there. He must have realised its potential and remembered its colour scheme of malachite and oxblood, which forms the key to his own work.

The portrait was completed in the summer of 1758, by when Ramsay had his portrait of Lord Bute well under way and had almost finished a full-length of his son, Lord Mount Stuart [*102*]. But Ramsay's father, the poet, had died in the first week of the year, and by 12 August, when he wrote the Earl the following letter, he had found it necessary to abandon these important commissions to travel north to wind up his father's estate:

Ramsay painted three portraits of the 3rd Duke of Argyll. A three-quarter-length standing in legal robes (Scottish National Portrait Gallery), which was engraved in 1744; a full-length of 1749 painted for Glasgow Town Council (Glasgow Art Gallery and Museums); and this seated three-quarter-length of 1758. David Martin, Ramsay's assistant in the late 1750s and 1760s, painted several versions of this last portrait. The Duke was the uncle of the 3rd Earl of Bute. They jointly owned Kenwood House until 1746, when Lord Bute bought his uncle's share. Later Lord Bute sold Kenwood to the uncle of Allan Ramsay's wife, the Lord Chancellor Lord Mansfield.

133

102

ALLAN RAMSAY

John, Lord Mount Stuart, later 1st
Marquess of Bute (1744–1814)

Signed and dated: A Ramsay 1759
Oil on canvas
93 x 58 (236.2 x 147.3)
Private collection

*The sitter was the son and heir of Ram-
say's great patron, the 3rd Earl of Bute.
He was educated at Harrow and is shown
wearing the uniform of the Harrow
archers, holding his prize, a silver arrow.
Although dated 1759, sittings took place
earlier, probably around the time of Lord
Mount Stuart's fourteenth birthday in
June 1758.*

134

'My Lord the confusion of my poor affairs in Scotland,
which instead of clearing, is daily becoming more con-
fused by the management of those to whom I have
entrusted the care of them, obliges me to write so many,
hitherto, ineffectual letters, that I run the hazard of losing
my health, if I do not put a stop to it. For that purpose, as
soon as I should have finished your Lordship's picture, I
proposed to have made a journey to Scotland; but find
now, besides other reasons against my delay, that it would
cast my journey very near the time my wife is expected to
ly in; a time when the care of her and of my family
demands my presence, in a particular manner at home.

'As I do not intend to paint a single stroak in Scotland, and shall lose no time upon the road, I still hope to have the picture finished by the end of September as I said to the Prince of Wales, having already made the studies for the hands and other necessary preparations; but could not, however, leave London without begging your Lordship's favour in my behalf; being of nothing so fearfull as of seeming inattentive to the commands with which his Royal Highness has been pleased to honour me.

'I am with the greatest respect, My Lord
'Your Lordship's most obliged and most
humble servant
Allan Ramsay

'P.S. The Prince of Wales's picture is dry enough to be transported if necessary; but I must beg leave to represent to your Lordship that, till it is put into its frame and hung upon a hook, it is no where safe but in my house, where my student and the rest of my family are well instructed not to suffer any body to approach it without proper caution, and to guard it from copiers and print makers. I have seen too many fatal accidents befall loose picture[s] in unskilfull hands, not to be anxious about one that has procured me so much notice.

'Lord Mount Stewart's picture is what I may call finished, but I intend to give it a revival; when it is thoroughly dry; which it will be by the time I return to London. My wife will take care of the collar, and your Lordship may have it anytime, if you have occasion for it.'[36]

The collar referred to must be Lord Mount Stuart's lace collar, which he wears as part of the uniform of a Harrow archer. As in the portrait of the Prince, Ramsay was able to convey the child's vulnerability and grace, choosing as his source not an antique marble but an insignificant print by Salvator Rosa which he had copied as a boy himself at the Academy of St Luke in Edinburgh. Lord Bute's portrait is the grandest of the three [97]. Like the pose of the Prince, which Batoni had used and which Louis Tocqué also adopted, Lord Bute's elegant stance also had fashionable international currency, having been chosen again by Tocqué for his contemporary portrait of Nikita Demidoff. Ramsay's colouring and technique also link his work to continental portraiture, particularly the work of French and Swiss pastelists like La Tour and Liotard, the latter admired by Lord Bute and the Royal Family.

No one seeing these magnificent full-lengths in the original can doubt that Ramsay deserved to be one of the King's Painters, the position to which he was appointed in December 1761, a year after the Prince had acceded to the

Fig. 21
The dining room at Lansdowne House, Berkeley Square, London. Robert Adam designed what later became known as Landsdowne House for the 3rd Earl of Bute. Metropolitan Museum of Art, Rogers Fund, 1932 (32.12)

throne as King George III. Reynolds's whale-like image of the King's uncle, the Duke of Cumberland, begun in 1758, can only have confirmed Ramsay's superiority in the eyes of the royal family. That he was not immediately made Principal Painter to His Majesty was due entirely to an untypical oversight on Ramsay's part in not soliciting for the post at the time of the accession. It went by default to the former holder, John Shackleton.

With his former pupil as King, Lord Bute's power and influence increased enormously. Hitherto Robert Adam had complained that the Earl had been unwilling to help him, but as soon as he could, Lord Bute made Adam one of the two newly created Architects of the King's Works, with an annual salary of £300. By 1762, when Bute officially became Prime Minister, Robert Adam was commissioned to build his town house on the south side of Berkeley Square [fig. 21]. In 1766 Adam began work for the Earl at Luton Hoo.

Ramsay, the author of philosophical papers and political commentaries, was a notable figure in intellectual circles. He was the friend of Hume, the correspondent of Diderot and the man about whom Dr Johnson remarked: 'I love Ramsay. You will not find a man in whose conversation there is more instruction, more information, and more elegance, than in Ramsay's.' His fluency in German, as well as French and Italian, eased his way at the Hanoverian court.

Ramsay painted the coronation portrait of King George III and its companion of the new Queen Charlotte of Mecklenburg-Strelitz; he painted their profiles for the coinage and from his studio, with David Martin as his chief assistant, very many versions of all of them; he

103
ALLAN RAMSAY
Augusta, Princess of Wales
(1719–72)
Oil on canvas
93 x 58 (236.2 x 147.3)
Private collection

painted the King's mother, the dowager Princess of Wales, walking on the terrace at Windsor [*103*] and he painted Queen Charlotte and her two eldest sons in a domestic yet dignified portrait of the Queen as mother, her work basket propped up on a volume of Locke on education [*104*]. So much was Ramsay now the painter of the Royal Family and their Prime Minister that Laurence Sterne wittily observed: 'Mr Ramsay, you paint only the court cards, the King, Queen and Knave.'

Sterne's remark recalls the widespread English hostility and abuse which was directed against the Prime Minister and by extension against successful Scots in London whom he was thought to have favoured. This alone

Augusta was the wife of Frederick, Prince of Wales, the eldest son of George II. The Earl and Countess of Bute were part of their circle. Frederick's early death in 1751 caused his widow to rely increasingly on Lord Bute's advice. He became her close friend and the tutor of her son George, now Prince of Wales himself. This portrait appears to have been commissioned by Lord Bute shortly after the death of George II in 1760, when Augusta's son, and Lord Bute's pupil, acceded to the throne as King George III.

104

ALLAN RAMSAY

Queen Charlotte (1744–1818) with
Her Two Eldest Sons

Oil on canvas
98 x 63¾ (248.9 x 161.9)
By Gracious Permission of Her
Majesty The Queen

This beautiful and dignified picture is remarkable for a state portrait in that it is Charlotte's role as a mother rather than queen that is emphasised. She appears to have been interrupted while playing with her children, a volume of John Locke's Some Thoughts concerning Education *conveniently close at hand. From the ages of the children the portrait would seem to have been painted in the mid-1760s, though Ramsay did not receive his payment of two hundred guineas until 1769. The boys are George, Prince of Wales, later George IV, and Prince Frederick, the children after whom Princes Street in Edinburgh was named.*

probably dissuaded Ramsay from accepting the knight-hood which could surely have been his, particularly after the death of John Shackleton in 1767, when the position of Principal Painter to His Majesty so effortlessly fell into his lap.

Ramsay had certainly been fortunate in Lord Bute's patronage. He acknowledged it warmly in a private letter he wrote in March that year. But he had benefited too from the constant interest of the Dukes of Argyll and from the patronage of Scotsmen like Lord Milton in Edinburgh, the Earl of Fife at Duff House, Sir James Grant of Grant and the Earl of Leven and Melville, all of whom sat to him. The Royal Family had been his greatest patrons and Ramsay served them too with the greatest distinction.

Notes

1 *Calendar of Treasury Papers 1556–1696* (xxiv).

2 *The Glamis Book of Record*, Scottish History Society, Edinburgh, 1890, vol IX, p. 105.

3 *Chronicles of the Atholl and Tullibardine Families*, Edinburgh, 1908, vol I, pp. 441–2.

4 *Colectanea de rebus Albanicis* (Iona Club): Edinburgh, 1847, Appendix, pp. 39–40.

5 *Reliquiae Hearnianae: The Remains of Thomas Hearne*, ed. Philip Bliss, 1857, vol I, p. 345.

6 George Vertue Notebooks: The Walpole Society, vol XVIII, 1929–30 (Vertue I), p. 48.

7 Scottish Record Office, GD 26/13/270/1.

8 Scottish Record Office, GD 18/4595.

9 Robertson Aikman Manuscripts: letter from William Aikman to Thomas Aikman of the Ross, 1/5/1707.

10 National Library of Scotland, Saltoun Papers, MS 16734.

11 Scottish Record Office, GD 18/4578.

12 Scottish Record Office, GD 18/4595.

13 Scottish Record Office, GD 18/4585.

14 William Fraser, *The Chiefs of Grant*, 1883, vol I, p. 327.

15 James Robertson, *General View of the Agriculture in the County of Inverness, 1808*, p. LVI.

16 George Vertue Notebooks: The Walpole Society, vol XXII, 1933–4 (Vertue III), p. 36.

17 ibid., p. 161.

18 Scottish Record Office, GD 345/1156/5/item 50.

19 Historical Manuscripts Commission: *Stuart Papers at Windsor*, vol VI, p. 561.

20 Historical Manuscripts Commission: *Stuart Papers at Windsor*, vol VII, p. 5.

21 ibid., p. 50.

22 Scottish Record Office, RH/15/1/145.

23 Scottish Record Office, GD 18/4610.

24 Craigston Muniments, Bundle 72, William Mosman to Captain John Urquhart, 5/11/1736.

25 Scottish National Portrait Gallery, 887 and 888.

26 Craigston Muniments, Bundle 72, William Mosman to Captain John Urquhart, 25/9/1733.

27 ibid., William Mosman to Captain John Urquhart, 17/10/1734.

28 Quoted in W. Dunlap, *A History of the Rise and Progress of the Arts of Design in the United States*, 1834, p. 165.

29 The document is published in full with the complete list of signatories in R. Brydall, *Art in Scotland*, 1889, pp. 110, 111.

30 *A letter from a Gentleman in Town to his friend in the country relating to the Royal Infirmary* (Philasthenes), 1739.

31 National Library of Scotland, Saltoun Papers, MS 16709.

32 *Memoirs of James Caulfield, Earl of Charlemont*, ed. Francis Hardy, 1810, p. 8.

33 National Library of Scotland, Saltoun Papers, MS 16703.

34 Alastair Smart, *The Life and Art of Allan Ramsay*, 1952, pp. 29, 30.

35 *A Prime Minister and his son*, ed. the Hon. Mrs E. Stuart Wortley, C.B.E., 1925, pp. 13, 14.

36 Private archive. Letter of Allan Ramsay to John, 3rd Earl of Bute, 12/8/1758.

Artists' biographies

WILLIAM AIKMAN (1682–1731)

A graduate of the University of Edinburgh, Aikman became a painter with the encouragement of his uncle Sir John Clerk of Penicuik [5]. He trained under Medina in Edinburgh and was in London between 1704 and 1707, when he left for Italy. He returned to Scotland in 1711, painting portraits such as Lady Grisel Baillie [39]. With the encouragement of the Duke of Argyll, Aikman in 1723 settled in London, where he mixed with Alexander Pope and other literary figures and painted portraits of Lord Burlington, Sir Robert Walpole and many Scotsmen. He was painting the Royal Family for Lord Burlington in 1730 when his health deteriorated. He died the following year.

BIBLIOGRAPHY

Holloway, J.E., *William Aikman* (Scottish Masters 9), Edinburgh, 1988.

Wilton-Ely, J., 'Lord Burlington and The Virtuoso Portrait', *Architectural History*, vol 27: 1984.

COSMO ALEXANDER (1724–72)

The son of the painter John Alexander. Cosmo's first recorded work dates from 1742, a copy of George Jamesone's portrait of George, 5th Earl Marischal. Three years later he painted George Middleton. In that year too, he took up arms for Prince Charles Edward Stewart and subsequently fled abroad. Until 1751 Cosmo Alexander lived in Rome, painting members of the Jacobite community in the city. In 1751 he left Rome via Bologna and Venice for Paris, where he also painted members of the Scottish community. Alexander was in London by 1754, when he inherited the house of the architect James Gibbs, a fellow Aberdonian and Roman Catholic. The following year he was employed by the Town Council of Aberdeen to paint portraits of the Earl and Countess of Findlater. During the late 1750s and early 1760s Alexander appears to have moved between London and Scotland, painting portraits in both places. In 1763 he crossed to Holland. He was fined in The Hague for not paying his dues to the guild of painters (the confrérie). In 1765 in London he showed a portrait at the 6th annual exhibition of the Society of Artists from an address in Gerrard Street, Soho. The following year Alexander was in America, painting portraits of the Scottish community in Philadelphia, before moving north to New York in 1767. During the winter of 1768–9 he stayed with the governor of New Jersey, William Franklin, and then moved on to Newport, Rhode Island. With Gilbert Stuart as his assistant he

BIBLIOGRAPHY

Geddy, P. McL., 'Cosmo Alexander's travels and patrons in America', *Antiques* 112, November 1977.

Goodfellow, G.M., *The Art, life and times of Cosmo Alexander*, MA Thesis, Oberlin, Ohio, 1961.

Goodfellow, G.M., 'Cosmo Alexander in America', *Art Quarterly* XXVI, Autumn 1963.

Goodfellow, G.M., 'Cosmo Alexander in Holland', *Oud Holland* LXXIX (1964), 1, 85.

toured the southern states before returning to Scotland in 1771, the year before his death.

Painters

JOHN ALEXANDER (1686–c.1766)

John Alexander was working in London in 1710 and painted his self-portrait in miniature the following year at Leghorn, *en route* for Rome (Scottish National Portrait Gallery). There he painted portraits of British tourists, including Lord Chief Justice Coke (1714), and he appears to have studied under Chiari. He worked for the Jacobite Earl of Mar and for the exiled Stewart court, made several engravings after Raphael, and returned to Scotland in 1720. The same year Alexander began the staircase ceiling at Gordon Castle for the Duke of Gordon. He was based in Edinburgh. He married in 1723 and his son Cosmo was born the following year. In 1728 he engraved George Jamesone's self-portrait with his wife and child (Jamesone was Alexander's maternal grandfather). In 1729 Alexander signed the Charter of the Edinburgh Academy of St Luke. His surviving work of the 1730s suggests that he may have operated from Aberdeen as well as Edinburgh. He was out in the '45 and declared a wanted man in 1746 but he was back working openly by 1748. At the time of his death he was painting the Escape of Mary, Queen of Scots, from Loch Leven Castle. The landscape in this picture was painted from nature.

JAMES BRODIE (*fl.* 1736–8)

Only seven portraits are known by James Brodie and all represent members of the Brodie family. Of these, five are dated between 1736 and 1738. The artist may have been a son of Ludovick Brodie of Whytfield, Writer to the Signet, and his wife, Helen Grant. The father and three of his children – John or Ian, Francis, the well-known Edinburgh cabinet-maker, and Helen [74] – were painted by James Brodie.

JEREMIAH DAVISON (c. 1695–1745)

Born in London, the son of Scottish parents, Davison was one of a number of artists there (Allan Ramsay was another) who used the services of the drapery painter Joseph van Aken. He painted Frederick, Prince of Wales, in 1730 and Anna Maria Poyntz in 1735 (Althorp). A year later, having met the Duke of Atholl at a Masonic lodge, he was encouraged north and settled in Edinburgh. The Atholl family remained his constant patrons and through them he received commissions from Murray kinsmen and

141

other families, particularly in Perthshire. The two superb full-length marriage portraits of James and Christian Moray of Abercairney cost thirty-two guineas each in 1737. The Graemes of Inchbrackie, the Mercers of Aldie and the Murrays of Ochtertyre employed him later in the decade. In 1740 Davison painted the large group portrait of the Earl of Morton and his family [79]. He moved back to London before his death, which took place at his house in Leicester Fields in December 1745.

WILLIAM DELACOUR (*fl.* from 1740; died 1767)

BIBLIOGRAPHY

Fleming, J., 'Enigma of a rococo artist', *Country Life*, 24 May 1962, pp. 1224–6.

Fraser-Harris, D.F., 'William De la Cour, painter, engraver and teacher of drawing', *The Scottish Bookman*, vol I, No. 5, 1936.

Simpson, J., 'Lord Alemoor's villa at Hawkhill', *Bulletin of the Scottish Georgian Society*, 1972, vol I, pp. 2–9.

Probably born in France, or in London of French, possibly Huguenot, parents, Delacour worked as a portrait painter and theatre designer, living close to Covent Garden. In 1740 he painted the scenery for G. B. Pescetti's opera *Busiri*, and during the 1740s he published eight *Books of Ornament* of rococo motifs for the use of fellow designers and craftsmen. His portraits were in pastel (Tommy Stone, 1750) as well as oil. In 1753 he was in Dublin, having moved from Ormonde Quay to College Green. By 1757 Delacour had settled in Edinburgh, where he remained until his death ten years later. In Scotland he again painted portraits and worked in the Glasgow and Edinburgh theatres, but he also painted pure landscapes in watercolour and oil and undertook several decorative schemes. In 1760 he became the first master of the Trustees Academy and in 1764 some of the drawings of foliage which he had made for his students were sent to Aberdeen to the academy which Lord Deskford and others had founded with William Mosman as master.

WILLIAM DENUNE (*c.* 1712–50)

In 1729 Denune signed the Charter of the Edinburgh Academy of St Luke. His earliest known portrait, of the Rev. Archibald Gibson, dates from 1735. There follows a succession of dated portraits until his death in Dumfries in 1750. From the detailed inventories made of the paintings in his two studios in Edinburgh and Dumfries at the time of his death (Scottish Record Office, Edinburgh Register of Testaments), it appears that the artist had a portrait practice in the capital and in the south-west. A sale of his unclaimed portraits took place in Dumfries in May 1751, a second in Edinburgh in December 1751. Denune's grandest patron was the Duke of Hamilton, who paid him ten guineas for his portrait in 1746. The painter is probably the person referred to in Douglas's *Baronage of Scotland* under the entry for Denune of Catbole: '*William*

Denune Esq, a youth of great hopes and spirit, who died in the flower of his age, unmarried.'

DAVID DES GRANGES (1611–71/2)

Des Granges was a Channel Islander who became an engraver, miniaturist and painter in oils. Both Charles I and Charles II were his patrons; he was with the latter in Scotland in 1650 and 1651, when he was appointed His Majesty's Limner. In 1671, an old and ill man, he petitioned the King for payment for work done in Scotland. His death probably followed soon after, for although his claim was accepted no record of payment can be found.

BIBLIOGRAPHY

Long, B., *British Miniaturists (1520–1860)*, London, 1929.
Murdoch, J., *et al.*, *The English Miniature*, New Haven, Conn., 1982.

WILLIAM GOUW FERGUSON (1632/3–after 1695)

Ferguson was born in Scotland, where he is said to have received training. His earliest known work (Leningrad, Hermitage Museum) is dated 1650. During the 1660s he was living in The Hague. By 1681 he had moved to Batavier Straat, Amsterdam, and in that year he married a Swedish woman, Sara van Someren. His last dated works were painted in 1684 (London, Tate Gallery; National Gallery of Scotland). Vertue records that he travelled in Italy and France and came back to Britain at the end of his life. He is believed to have died after 1695.

DAVID MARTIN (1737–97)

Born in Anstruther, Martin became Allan Ramsay's assistant and joined him in Italy in 1755. When Ramsay secured royal favour, Martin, as his chief assistant and copyist, produced many of the state portraits which now, as then, go under Ramsay's name. In his turn Martin received royal patronage. In 1785, after his return to Edinburgh, he was created Portrait Painter to the Prince of Wales. Martin dominated portraiture in the city until the emergence of Raeburn.

SIR JOHN DE MEDINA (1659–1710)

Born in Brussels of a Spanish father, Medina trained under François Duchâtel, then moved to London in 1686 where he had a successful practice as a portrait painter. He also made illustrations for Ovid's *Metamorphoses* and Milton's *Paradise Lost*, the latter published by Jacob Tonson. In 1691 he painted the portraits of the Earl of Leven and his parents, the Earl and Countess of Melville, and as a result of their encouragement and patronage he moved to

BIBLIOGRAPHY

Fleming, J., 'Sir John Medina and his "Postures" ', *Connoisseur* CXLVIII, August 1961.
Mannings, D., 'Sir John Medina's portraits of the surgeons of Edinburgh', *Medical History*, 23, April 1979.
Marshall, R. K., *John de Medina* (Scottish Masters 7), Edinburgh, 1988.

Edinburgh in the winter of 1693–4. There he pursued a very successful career as a portrait painter; he also painted figure compositions, though these are much less well known today. Several are at Penicuik House; a painting of Cleopatra is also recorded. He was knighted in 1707. The list of paintings in his studio at the time of his death was published by Marshall (op. cit.). Many of them were still in the possession of his widow, Jean Mary Vandale, when she advertised their sale in the Scots *Courant* (4–14 May 1711). She was moving from her lodging on the second storey of the first fore-land above the Tron Church following the death of her husband seven months earlier.

WILLIAM MILLAR (*fl.* 1751–84)

William Millar is known to have worked in Edinburgh from 1751 to 1784. His earliest known painting is a copy after a Ramsay portrait of the 3rd Duke of Argyll which is dated 1751. He also copied portraits by Gavin Hamilton in the 1760s. Millar's own portraits are not without quality. They grow out of the style of Denune, later showing the influence of David Martin, who was his competitor in Edinburgh from 1767.

WILLIAM MOSMAN (*c.* 1700–1771)

Mosman was probably born in Aberdeen, where his brother Thomas later practised as an advocate. In 1727 he was in London, hoping to assist William Aikman. Four years later he was working at Culter House, Peterculter, for Patrick Duff of Premnay. Mosman was in Rome from at least January 1732 to December 1735, when he studied under Imperiali and acted as an agent for several Scottish collectors. He was in Leghorn in November 1736 and back in Aberdeen during the second half of 1738, when he painted the portraits of Patrick Duff and other members of his family. A sale of the collection he had assembled in Italy took place in Edinburgh in 1740, when advertisements announced that he was leaving the city. However, Mosman appears to have remained in Edinburgh during the 1740s: the records of the Episcopal Chapel of St Paul's, Carrubber's Close, attest to his presence in the city in 1743, 1744 and 1745. The portraits of Sir Thomas Kennedy of 1746 [72] and John Campbell of the Bank of 1749 [83] are likely to have been painted in Edinburgh. The undated *Macdonald Boys* (Scottish National Portrait Gallery) is likely to be a work by Mosman of the late 1740s.

In the early 1750s Mosman may have moved north. The View of Aberdeen of 1756 [73] and a full-length portrait of Robert Gordon of 1758, as well as his work repairing busts for the library at Monymusk in 1759 and designing figures after Raphael and Maratta for the Grants' burialplace, suggest that Mosman had made Aberdeen his home. He was teaching drawing there in the early 1760s, being supplied from Edinburgh in 1764 with drawings of foliage by Delacour. Apart from a meticulous red chalk copy of Kneller's portrait of Bishop Burnet, nothing further is known of his work of the 1760s. Mosman died in Aberdeen in November 1771.

DAVID MURRAY (*fl.* 1733)

It is not at all certain that David Murray really was an artist. He is associated with only two paintings: [48] and a larger but almost identical version at the New Club, Edinburgh, which differs from it only in that Murray's name and the date 1733 are missing from the cartouche. It is possible that Murray was the master of the hounds shown in the pictures.

JAMES NORIE (SENIOR) (1684–1757)

Born at Knockando but moved to Edinburgh, where his father was described as a merchant. In 1709 he was admitted freeman of the Incorporated Trades of Edinburgh, St Mary's Chapel, and two years later Alexander Miller, the first of a number of apprentices, was working for him. In 1718 he painted the chimney piece in the convening house of St Mary's Chapel and during that year and the following was working for the Earl of Hopetoun. Norie was a friend of Allan Ramsay and in 1721 subscribed to the first edition of his poems. During the twenties he worked further at Hopetoun and also at Marchmont. In 1729 he signed the Charter establishing the Academy of St Luke. There are a number of dated canvases from the thirties. The earliest, of 1731, now lost, was at Newhall, Carlops. It is difficult to know whether canvases signed James Norie are by the father or the son. In 1736 he lived opposite Blackfriars Wynd Head in Edinburgh. In 1743 he became a deacon of the Wrights. In the late forties his firm was working for the government at Fort William and in 1750 at Fort Augustus and Edinburgh Castle. He was paid five guineas in 1753 for painting the organ at St Cecilia's Hall. In 1754 he sketched a coat of arms for Robert Adam. A view of Melrose is inscribed on the back 'James Norie 1757', the year he died. He was buried in Greyfriars Churchyard.

BIBLIOGRAPHY
Anon., *James Norie* (privately printed), 1890.

JAMES NORIE (JUNIOR) (1711–36)

The eldest son of James Norie (Senior), he signed the Charter of the Academy of St Luke in 1729. His father sent him and his brother Robert to London, where they trained under George Lambert. No work indisputably by him can be identified, but a case can be made for attributing the signed and dated canvases of the early 1730s to the son rather than the father, as is customary.

BIBLIOGRAPHY

Holloway, J., 'Robert Norie in London and Perthshire', *Connoisseur*, January 1978.

DAVID PATON (*fl.* from 1668; died after 1708)

Paton was the leading miniature painter in Scotland in the seventeenth century. He also painted portraits in oils. In the late 1670s he was in Italy accompanying William Tollemache, the youngest son of the Duchess of Lauderdale, on his grand tour. There he came to the attention of Duke Cosimo III de'Medici, whose correspondence shows that Paton had moved from Scotland to London at the beginning of the eighteenth century and that he was still alive in 1708, when he drew the portrait of Sir Isaac Newton which was sent by the Tuscan ambassador in London to Duke Cosimo III.

BIBLIOGRAPHY

Crino, A.M., 'Documents relating to some portraits in the Uffizi and to a portrait at Knole', *Burlington Magazine*, vol CII, June 1960.
Foskett, D., *Miniatures: Dictionary and Guide*, Antique Collectors' Club, 1987.
Long, B., *British Miniaturists (1520–1860)*, London, 1929.

ALLAN RAMSAY (1713–84)

Born in Edinburgh, the son of Allan Ramsay the poet, the artist trained first at the Academy of St Luke in Edinburgh, then under Hans Hysing in London, and finally under Imperiali and Solimena in Rome and Naples. By 1739 he was established in Covent Garden, but he made periodic visits to Edinburgh, where he maintained a studio in his father's house. Soon after a visit to Rome in the company of Robert Adam, Ramsay, through the influence of the 3rd Earl of Bute, painted the portrait of the Prince of Wales [*100*]. After the latter's accession in 1760, Ramsay became King George III's court painter, a position which was confirmed seven years later when he became Principal Painter to His Majesty. Shortly after a third visit to Italy (1775–7) Ramsay broke his arm, making it impossible for him to paint, but his career as an essayist and political commentator continued. He died at Dover on his return from a fourth visit to Italy.

BIBLIOGRAPHY

Brown, I.G., 'Allan Ramsay's Rise and Reputation', *The Walpole Society*, vol L, 1984.
Brown, I.G., 'Young Allan Ramsay in Edinburgh', *Burlington Magazine*, vol CXXVI, December 1984.
Brown, I.G., *Poet and Painter: Allan Ramsay, father and son, 1684–1784*, National Library of Scotland, Edinburgh, 1985.
Brown, I.G., 'The Pamphlets of Allan Ramsay the younger', *The Book Collector*, vol 37, No. 1, Spring 1988.
Caw, J., 'Allan Ramsay, Portrait Painter 1713–1784', *The Walpole Society*, vol XXV, 1937.
Fleming, J., 'Allan Ramsay and Robert Adam in Italy', *Connoisseur*, vol CXXXVII, March 1956.
Holloway, J.E., 'Two projects to illustrate Allan Ramsay's treatise on Horace's Sabine villa', *Master Drawings*, vol 14, No. 3, 1976.
Sanderson, K., 'Engravings after Allan Ramsay', *The Print Collector's Quarterly*, vol 18, No. 2, April 1931.

Smart, A., *The Life and Art of Allan Ramsay*, London, 1952.
Smart, A., *Paintings and Drawings by Allan Ramsay* (exhibition catalogue), Kenwood and Nottingham University, 1958.
Smart, A., *Allan Ramsay* (exhibition catalogue), Royal Academy, London, 1964.
Smart, A., 'A Newly Discovered Portrait of Allan Ramsay's Second Wife', *Apollo*, vol CXIII, May 1981.

WILLIAM ROBERTSON (*fl.* 1727–83)

Active in Edinburgh between 1727, when he signed and dated a portrait of his future father-in-law, Charles Steuart, and 1783, when he is recorded as living in Old Playhouse Close. In 1729 he signed the Charter establishing the Edinburgh Academy of St Luke. In 1753 he was named a debtor seeking refuge in the Abbey Sanctuary. Robertson (who signed his name Robinson on occasion) has a distinctive feathery, insubstantial style. He appears to have been patronised in particular by families, like the Oliphants of Gask, who had Jacobite sympathies. He is also known for his portraits of the Young Pretender and Flora Macdonald.

WILLIAM ROSS (*fl.* 1753)

Nothing is known of the artist apart from a single signed and dated portrait [75].

DAVID SCOUGAL (*fl.* 1654–77)

The portrait of Lady Jean Campbell [3] is David Scougal's only signed painting; it is also dated, 1654. Normally, with a seventeenth-century artist, further attributions can be made from references to payments in contemporary documents, but in David Scougal's case this is difficult. Bills very often refer to 'Mr Scougal' or 'Old Scougal', neither of which names can be assumed to refer to David Scougal. However, a tentative chronology can be established by identifying the better-documented works of the younger artist John Scougal and grouping the remaining early Scougal portraits together and attributing them to the older artist. David Scougal then emerges as a distinctive and talented artist, whose early work of the 1650s is represented at its best by the portraits of Lady Jean Campbell and her father, the Marquis of Argyll [2]. The excellent pair of portraits of Sir John and Lady Clerk of Penicuik are late works [5, 7].

JOHN SCOUGAL (*c.* 1645–1737)

Probably the son or nephew of David Scougal, with whom he is likely to have trained. He married in Aberdeen in 1680. Documents list portraits by him from 1675, but it is very difficult to be certain to which portraits they refer. One of the earliest is the oval portrait of the 4th Earl of Panmure at Glamis, which appears to date from 1689. The pair of portraits of Sir Francis and Lady Grant [34, 35] is documented to 1700. John Scougal was recorded as a limner in Edinburgh in 1690 and

BIBLIOGRAPHY
Anon., in *Scottish Art Review*, vol IV-1, 1952.

had premises and a picture gallery on the east side of Advocates' Close. Between 1693 and 1702 he copied portraits for Glasgow University at a guinea each. He painted portraits of King William and Queen Mary (for Glasgow Town Council, March 1708, purchase approved) and Queen Anne, for which he was paid £15 in 1712. He retired in 1715. In 1744, seven years after his death, his collection of paintings was valued by William Mosman.

JOHN SMIBERT (1688–1751)

Born in Edinburgh, where he was apprenticed to Walter Marshall. He travelled to London in 1709 and studied at Kneller's Great Queen Street Academy. He spent the years between 1716 and 1719 in Edinburgh and then visited Italy. He returned to London in 1722, staying there until 1728, when he left for America. The following year he settled in Boston, Massachusetts, where he died in 1751. Smibert's main business was portrait painting, occasionally in miniature. The drawing he holds in his hand in the Bermuda Group (Yale University Art Gallery) suggests that he may have painted landscapes as well. He was the architect of Faneuil Hall in Boston.

BIBLIOGRAPHY

Foote, H.W., *John Smibert, Painter*, Cambridge, Mass., 1950.
Massachusetts Historical Society, *The Notebook of John Smibert*, Boston, Mass., 1969.
Riley, S.T., 'John Smibert and the business of Portrait Painting', in *American Painting to 1776: A Reappraisal*, Charlottesville, Virginia, 1971.
Saunders, R.H., *John Smibert (1688–1751), Anglo-American Portrait Painter*, Ph.D. diss., Yale University, 1979.
Saunders, R.H., and E.G. Miles, *American Colonial Portraits 1700–1776* (exhibition catalogue), Washington D.C., 1987.
Yale University Art Gallery, *The Smibert Tradition: The first selected showing of John Smibert's Paintings since 1730* (exhibition catalogue), New Haven, Conn., 1949.

BIBLIOGRAPHY

Cheape, D.H.G., 'Portraiture in Piping', *The Scottish Pipe Band Monthly*, No. 6, January 1988.

RICHARD WAITT (*fl.* from 1708; died 1732)

Waitt was married in Edinburgh in 1707 and in the following year was paid for painting the Earl of Hopetoun's coat of arms at Abercorn Church. His earliest dated portrait is Mrs Boswell of 1709, after which there follows a succession of dated portraits until 1716. Between 1716 and 1722 nothing is known of Waitt, but for the rest of the 1720s dated works survive for all but two years. In 1730 he was paid thirty pounds for painting the arms of Great Britain in the Court House of Elgin. It is his last known work; he is said to have died two years later.

THOMAS WARRENDER (*fl.* 1673–1713)

In 1673 Thomas Warrender of Haddington was apprenticed in Edinburgh to John Tait, whose work is now unknown. Warrender became a burgess and guild brother in 1692, and later in that decade he was working independently at Hamilton Palace (imitation marbling, festoons of fruits and flowers etc., 1696–7), Cramond Kirk (commissioned by Lady Margaret Hope to paint and gild the Hope monument, 1697), and Craigie Hall (decorating bedrooms in 'olive wood colour and landscape work', and painting the Order of the Thistle on the Marquess of Annandale's coach, 1698–1705). In the early eighteenth century Warrender was at Hopetoun, where he was paid £171 Scots for painting 'all the pannells of the Countess bed cha^r in fyne landscape work of walnut tree collour in oyll and the styles Japand on etc'. He was also paid £360 Scots 'For collouring, marbelling, varnishing, and guilding with fyne Inglish gold, all the requisite parts of ye sd princl staircase, and whitening most of the plaster of it, and collouring all the top of the cupilla anen once over w^t a stone of glass collours in oyll.' In 1704 he was paid £44 for painting and gilding 28 batons belonging to the constables of Edinburgh. After 1710 his son John continued his family business. The still-life [*44*] is the only work by Thomas Warrender known to exist.

JACOB DE WET (1640–97)

Born in Haarlem, the son of a painter, de Wet was brought to Scotland in about 1673 by Sir William Bruce to work at the Palace of Holyroodhouse. He was employed by Bruce at his own house, Balcaskie, in 1674, and a year or two later at Kellie Castle, also in Fife. De Wet appears to have returned to the Continent in September 1677, when he became a member of the Painters' Corporation of Cologne, but he was back in Scotland at least by February 1684, when, described as 'In dwellar in the cannongate' and styled as 'His majesties pictur drawer in Scotland', he signed the contract to paint the series of kings for Holyroodhouse. He worked for the Duke of Hamilton in 1685, and in January 1688 signed the contract to paint a large number of works for the Earl of Strathmore at Glamis. De Wet was back in Haarlem in 1691 and died in Amsterdam six years later.

JOHN MICHAEL WRIGHT (1617–94)

Born in London on 25 May 1617, possibly to Scottish parents. He was in Edinburgh, apprenticed to George Jamesone, from 1636 to 1641. Perhaps during the following year he went to Rome, where he became the only British painter of the century to be elected a member of the Accademia di San Luca. By 1650 Wright was (if he had not always been) a Roman Catholic. He was also an antiquary as well as a painter and printmaker. In 1653 or 1654 he left Italy for a post in Flanders as antiquary to

BIBLIOGRAPHY

Apted, M.R., 'The Glamis Bible', *Archaeolog* (The Royal Photographic Society of Great Britain, Archaeological Group), No. 12, December 1979.
Dunbar, J.G., 'Lowlanders in The Highlands: Dutch craftsmen in Restoration Scotland', *Country Life*, 8 August 1974.
Guilding, R.A., 'The De Wet Apostle paintings in the Chapel at Glamis Castle', *Proceedings of the Society of Antiquaries of Scotland*, vol 116, 1986.
Haverkorn van Rijswijk, P., 'De Schilder Jacob de Wet in Schotland', *Oud Holland*, XVII, 1899.

BIBLIOGRAPHY

Collins Baker, C.H., *Lely and the Stuart Portrait painters*, London, 1912.
Fenlon, J., 'John Michael Wright's "Highland Laird" identified', *Burlington Magazine*, vol CXXX, October 1988.
Stevenson, S., and D. Thomson, *John Michael Wright. The King's Painter* (exhibition catalogue), Edinburgh, 1982.

the Archduke Leopold, governor of the Spanish Netherlands. In April 1656 he landed at Dover, intending to return to Italy, but apparently remained in England, and in April 1659 he was described by Evelyn as 'the famous painter Mr Write'. After the Restoration of 1660 Wright won royal patronage, painting the Whitehall ceiling [8] and a St Catherine for the Queen's privy chamber. What little is known of his movements in the late 1660s and 1670s suggests that he remained based in London. In 1679 he is known to have been in Dublin, where he may have remained for four years, a time of bitter Roman Catholic persecution in England. He was back in London before joining the Earl of Castlemaine's embassy to Pope Innocent XI in 1685–6. He returned to London in 1687 and died there in 1694.

Select bibliography

Apted, M. R., and S. Hannabus, *Painters in Scotland 1301–1700*: A biographical dictionary. Scottish Record Society, New Series 7, Edinburgh, 1978.

Caw, J. L., *Scottish Painting Past and Present 1620–1908*, Edinburgh, 1908.

Croft-Murray, E., *Decorative Painting in England 1537–1837*, vols I & II, London, 1962, 1970.

Holloway, J. E., and L. M. Errington, *The Discovery of Scotland*, Edinburgh, 1978.

Irwin, D. and F., *Scottish Painters at Home and Abroad 1700–1900*, London, 1975.

MacMillan, D., *Painting in Scotland: The Golden Age*, Oxford, 1986.

Marshall, R. K., *Women in Scotland 1660–1780*, Edinburgh, 1979.

Skinner, B., *Scots in Italy in the C18*, Edinburgh, 1966.

Vertue, G., The Notebooks of George Vertue: The Walpole Society, vols XVIII, XX, XXII, XXIV, XXVI, XXIX and XXX (1929–50).

Waterhouse, E., *Painting in Britain 1530 to 1790*, Harmondsworth, 1953.

Waterhouse, E., *The Dictionary of British 18th Century Painters*, Woodbridge, 1981.

Waterhouse, E., *The Dictionary of British 16th and 17th Century Painters*, Woodbridge, 1988.

Index

Abercromby, James, 60
Adam family, 112
Adam, John, 118–20
Adam, Robert, 120, 130, 131, 136, 145, 146 [fig. 21]
Adam, William, 65–6, 93, 94, 96–9, 105, 108–9, 120 [figs. 17–18]
Aikman, William, 46, 47, 51–61, 62, 67, 74, 75, 81, 82, 92–3, 107, 126, 132, 140, 144 [36–42]
Alexander, Cosmo, 89, 101–3, 140–1 [76–8]
Alexander, John, 82, 85–92, 101, 103, 105, 108, 109, 112, 140, 141 [63–6, 80; fig. 15]
Allan, David, 116, 121

Batoni, Pompeo, 95, 131, 133, 135
Berchem, Nicholas, 106
Bianchi, Pietro, 95
Brodie, James, 99–100, 141 [74]
Bruce, Sir William, 23–4, 124, 149

Callot, Claude, 42
Chambers, 74
Chiari, Giuseppe Bartolomeo, 85, 86, 87, 88, 95, 141
Clérisseau, Charles Louis, 131
Clerk, Alexander, 105
Clerk of Eldin, John, 109, 112, 116
Closterman, John, 37
Collison, Jan, 42
Cooper, Richard, 98, 105, 106 [fig. 18]
Cortona, Pietro da, 19
Costanzi, Placido, 95, 101
Cruden, John, 42

Dandini, Pietro, 77
David, Antonio, 95, 98, 99
Davison, Jeremiah, 106–7, 141–2 [79]
Delacour, William, 109, 118–21, 142, 145 [81, 91–3; fig. 20]
Denune, William, 105, 112–14, 124, 142–3, 144 [86, 88]
Des Granges, David, 13–14, 143 [1]
Duchâtel, François, 33, 143
Duquesnoy, François, 106

Enzer, Joseph, 93

Faber, John, 126
Ferguson, William Gouw, 43–5, 142 [29–31; fig. 6]
Foggini, Giovanni Battista, 88

Giambologna, 40, 41
Gibbons, Grinling, 31, 37
Gibbs, James, 66–7, 97, 102, 140
Griffier, Jan II, 65

Hamilton, Ferdinand Phillipp, 42
Hamilton, Gavin, 144
Hamilton, James, 42, 43
Hamilton, Johann Georg, 42
Hamilton, Karl Wilhelm, 42
Hanneman, Adriaen, 13–14
Hay, Andrew, 78, 105
Hogarth, William, 123, 124, 126
Hysing, Hans, 123, 146

Imperiali, Francesco, 94, 95, 96, 98, 99, 124, 131, 144, 146

Jaffray, Alexander, 93
Jamesone, George, 18, 25, 83, 85, 140, 141, 149
Jervas, Charles, 59–60

Kent, William, 58–9, 85
Kirk, Thomas, 62
Kneller, Sir Godfrey, 33, 36, 37, 38, 39–40, 52, 58, 60, 91, 145, 148

Lambert, George, 63, 146
Lanark Painter, the, 46
La Tour, Maurice-Quentin de, 135
Lely, Sir Peter, 20, 22 [fig. 1]
Liotard, Jean-Etienne, 135

Maratta, Carlo, 54, 145
Marinari, Onorio, 77
Marshall, Walter, 75
Martin, David, 130, 131, 133, 136, 143, 144 [99]
Mazell, Peter, 31
Medina, John, junior, 42
Medina, Sir John de, 33–42, 45, 49, 51–2, 53, 54, 74, 78, 82, 140, 143–4 [20–8; fig. 5]
Mengs, Anton Rafael, 131
Mercier, Philip, 112
Millar, William, 112, 115, 144 [85]
Miller, Alexander, 145
Morgan, William, 31
Mosman, William, 85, 92–9, 110–13, 124, 142, 144–5, 148 [68–73, 83–4; fig. 16; frontispiece]
Murray, David, 64, 145 [48]
Murray, Thomas, 42

Natoire, Charles-Joseph, 131
Norie family, 93–4, 106, 112
Norie, James, senior, 60–6, 105, 120, 145–6 [43, (?) 45–7, 49, 50; figs. 10–11]
Norie, James, junior, 63, 64, 105, 145–6 [(?) 45–7, 49, 50]
Norie, Robert, 63, 120, 146

Ogilvie, George, 60

Panini, Giovanni, 62, 106
Parrocel, Etienne, 95
Paton, David, 22–3, 146 [12–13]
Perrier, François, 106

Ramsay, Allan, 77, 96, 105, 106, 112, 114–17, 118–20, 123–38, 141, 143, 144, 146 [82, 87, 89, 90, 94–8, 100–4]

Raphael, 86, 87, 88, 95, 109, 123, 141, 145
Reni, Guido, 85, 93, 95
Rennie, William, 26–7
Reynolds, Sir Joshua, 124, 129–30, 132, 136
Robertson, Charles, 112
Robertson, William, 105, 147 [58]
Romanelli, Giovanni Francesco, 77
Rosa, Salvator, 106, 135
Ross, George, 85
Ross, William, 99–101, 147 [75]
Roubiliac, Louis François, 67 [fig. 12]
Rubens, Peter Paul, 27, 87
Runciman, Alexander, 116, 121

Sacchi, Andrea, 19
Sandby, Paul, 109, 112–16 [fig. 19]
Santvoort, Jan van, 23
Schenck, Pieter, 39
Schunemann, L., 24
Scougal, David, 14–17, 33–4, 46, 147 [2–7]
Scougal, George, 61
Scougal, John, 17, 34, 45–9, 56, 61, 72, 76, 147–8 [32–5; fig. 7]
Shackleton, John, 136, 138
Slezer, John, 24
Smibert, John, 48, 74–81, 123, 148 [54–7]
Smith, James, 31, 39, 49 [fig. 8]
Smith, John, 91
Solimena, Francesco, 124, 146
Strange, Robert, 106
Stuart, Gilbert, 103, 104
Subleyras, Pierre, 124

Tait, John, 148
Talman, John, 54, 58
Titian, 87
Tocqué, Louis, 135
Trevisani, Francesco, 87, 95

Van Aelst, Willem, 45
Van Aken, Joseph, 141
Vanbrugh, Sir John, 78
Van Dyck, Sir Anthony, 14, 22
Visitella, Isaac, 14
Vogelsang, Isaak, 63
Volterrano, 77
Vorstermans, Johannes, 24

Waitt, Richard, 70–4, 80–3, 148 [51–2, 59–62; fig. 14]
Warrender, John, 62, 149
Warrender, Thomas, 61–2, 148–9 [44]
Watson, John, 73–4
Watteau, Antoine, 126
Weenix, Jan, 45
Westerhout, Aernout van, 20
Wet, Jacob de, 16, 17, 23–7, 28, 149 [15–17; figs. 2–3]
Wleughels, Nicolas, 124
Wright, John Michael, 14, 18–22, 23, 27–31, 33, 149–50 [8–11, 14, 18–19]
Wyck, Jan, 31

Lenders

Her Majesty The Queen 10, 36, 104
Aberdeen Art Gallery and Museums 47, 73, 76
Brodies, WS, Edinburgh 74
Sir John Clerk of Penicuik, Bt 5, 7, 17, 26, 27, 37
Charles Cottrell-Dormer 1
Dundee Art Gallery and Museums 31
Edinburgh, City Art Centre 81, 84
Edinburgh, National Gallery of Scotland 12, 28, 29, 44, 45, 46, 61, 63, 77, 78, 85, 87, 89, 98
Edinburgh, National Museums of Scotland 51
Edinburgh, Royal Infirmary 80
Edinburgh, Royal Scottish Academy 43
Edinburgh, Scottish National Portrait Gallery 2, 3, 13, 14, 18, 20, 21, 23, 38, 40, 49, 62, 79, 86, 88, 91, 94
Edinburgh, University 92
J. T. T. Fletcher of Saltoun 82
Government Art Collection 19
Sir Archibald Grant of Monimusk, Bt 34, 35, 54, 55, 57, 58
The Rt Honble the Earl of Haddington 24, 39
His Grace The Duke of Hamilton 64
Lt. Col. Sir John Inglefield-Watson, Bt 32, 33
The Kintore Trust 65, 66
The Rt Honble the Earl of Leven and Melville 22
London, National Portrait Gallery 95, 99
The National Trust for Scotland, The House of the Binns 48
The National Trust for Scotland, Bute House 97
The National Trust for Scotland, Culzean Castle 72
His Grace The Duke of Northumberland 101
Nottingham Castle Museum and Art Gallery 8
The Honble Viscount Reidhaven 52
Miss Elizabeth Rose of Kilravock 75
The Rt Honble the Earl of Rothes 6, 11
The Royal Bank of Scotland plc 83
The Royal Company of Archers 53
Mrs Oliver Russell 60
The Rt Honble the Earl of Seafield 16, 59
Charles G. Spence 41, 50
The Rt Honble the Earl of Wemyss and March, K.T. 9, 25, 67
Other private collections 4, 15, 30, 42, 56, 68, 69, 70, 71, 90, 93, 96, 100, 102, 103